On the Way to Over the Hill

A Guide to Aging gracefully

Grace Lee

Copyright © 1997 by Grace Lee

FIRST EDITION

Published by Educare Press
PO Box 75086
Seattle, WA 98125-0086

International Standard Book Number: 0-944638-11-2

Library of Congress Cataloging Card Number: 97-060077

Printed in the United States of America

10 9 8 7 6 5 4 3 2

Graphic design by Gloria Gorel
Cover design by Megan Haas

To my cousin Joyce Koenig who conceived of this book,
to Sue Gilbert who midwifed it.

Acknowledgements

The following are only a few of the many who offered singular encouragement along the highway. I must acknowledge Eleanor Welles, Joe and Rachelle Simon, Stacey Peck, Mitch Schorow, Miriam Boroff, and Gloria Gorel with special thanks. My editor and publisher Kieran O'Mahony owns my deep appreciation.

Preface

I have been writing about the new age of aging for more than ten years. Two of those years were devoted to a Q&A column entitled *"As We Age"* for the Gannett press.

It was a surprise for me to learn that readers in their 40's and 50's not only sent in questions about their parents but perused the columns for reasons of their own. Those in early middle years seem to be prematurely concerned with how to deal with their own aging.

At the last census 55, 659 citizens of these United States were counted as over 100 years of age. This population is expected to double by 2010. That's a good reason for those along the path to anticipate the latter years. There is already a healthy volume of reading material about how to survive middle-age. I would like to add to these an account of my own aging experiences.

Sincerely,

Grace Lee
Seattle, WA. January, 1997

Contents

Introduction

THE STATE OF GRACE

We are never fully prepared for aging. No matter how gracefully we set aside our youth or how vigorous the middle-years, it's a prickly path to elderly.

I have one sharp memory on the very edge of that migration. In the 19th year of my life, my image in the bathroom mirror seemed suddenly unfamiliar. I shouted for my parents. They rushed in only to hear me say, "Look at me. This face will wrinkle. Now it's pretty if only because it is smooth. I love being 19."

My parents stared at me and then at each other. They said nothing nor did their eyes meet again. Each went to a neutral corner. To what? To mourn their own short youth? To weep for a 19 year old who must also grow old and already understood this?

The comeliness of youth was set aside graciously. I prepared to mellow into my latter years with sense and style. I practiced proper diet and exercise to keep my waistline in line. When despite my best efforts, my weight shifted from petite to a next higher dress size and beyond anyway, I still did not require a Mother Hubbard cover-up. My aging shape was kept suitably chic with handsome scarves and hats.

When my eyes dimmed and print blurred, I wore fashion glasses. And strangely enough the first gray hairs were a welcome change because big time and money were no longer spent on counterfeit color. Perhaps most important I kept my mind supple with the challenge of bridge lessons and cross word puzzles and the body limber with aqua exercise and the latest dance steps. Some of them recycled from my other eras except what had been skipping and jumping could now be seen as limping and faltering. Although we ripen differently from one another there is hardly a senior person without a list of damages. Our arches can fall, our blood pressure can rise or our bladders can leak.

At 19, I had expected my waning years to be elegant and dignified. I would blossom like some exotic plant. Why not? All my other transitions had bettered me. My dreamy child turned into a lively adolescent, my young adulthood was filled with promise and middle-age had been surprisingly erotic. I had expected a mild winter season. More fool I!

Yet despite the penalties exacted by longevity, the last years can be some of the best.

The Japanese term for Senior Citizen is Harvest Time. That means we no longer have to work as hard because we work smart and often accomplish as much. Most of us have developed a sharp ability to rank activities. We are able to initiate a priority system which allows us to do only the important. We do what gives us satisfaction and leaves time for naps. Naps make growing old more relaxing than one might imagine. It is both restful and thrilling to still the alarm clock permanently.

The older person is giving a whole new meaning to aging in America. The last census counted more than 30 million of us over 65 years and 55, 679 centenarians. We stand taller and straighter than the generations before us. We also reach higher.

Given the choice between young and old, young is better in many ways. Older brains could use some younger, stronger bones to advantage. "Give us another chance" some of us chant. Well, we don't get another chance. This is it folks!

Each cycle was natural in its time. Of course, our stiff, aching joints or thinning hair are humbling. Finding ways to overcome it, ignore it or to bear it well is the big challenge. Some of us are content not to try. Some of us cannot. But for those of us who are able and willing to climb to a new summit, the thrill of living is not over. The following pages mark my trek "On the Way to Over the Hill." It takes a sure and steady ASCENT to a safe and secure PLATEAU and an eventual slow and easy DESCENT to complete the trip. There are roadblocks to be sure but the scenery along the way is highly recommended.

The Ascent

SOMEWHERE IN THE CONTINUUM

I was not depressed on my 70th birthday. I was in shock. Gerontology experts have classified "that age" as only young-old. That's because today's spectrum of aging leaves years and years beyond 70 for inhaling and exhaling. Nonetheless, I just stood there on the day I became young-old and shook. 70 is an astonishing number. It impressed me right down to my knocking knees. Not because it was scary but because it was such a surprise. I had not expected to live past 60.

A large part of me had already stopped living when I was 35. I became a widow that year. Ten months after our only child died, I struggled to find a reason for a life without them. Trance-like I enrolled in college. It had structure to fill my days and the promise of a future purpose. It was a good choice. I was an indifferent scholar but found a reason for my diplomas. I became teacher and social worker to parents and children who were strangers to me.

My emptiness was never quite filled but it grew tolerable. Not only was my work absorbing but a host of friends and relations enfolded me into their circle. In time I realized I had constructed a substitute life which held many satisfying years. And before I knew it there were 70 of them.

The trauma of reaching this major milestone subsided when I began to appreciate my assets at 70. My sense of sight, sound, smell, touch and taste are in operating order. My personality is more youthful than one could expect for my age and my walk still has spring. There is, however, a jolt or two to deal with. The first time I saw an older woman wearing my clothes in a department store mirror was one. I thought, "how odd, that woman is wearing my exact outfit." It took a few seconds to acknowledge that image as mine.

Of more consequence is my intense curiosity about the world. I think it is a canard that as we grow older we take a rigid stance in a belief system. I am among those 70 year olds who are examining our biases in light of recent events and new information. Women have entered every professional avenue since the days I had few options. Gays of both genders live in our neighborhood and are born to our families. Countries have been realigned in three continents. These facts have changed my attitudes. I used to think I knew all the answers. At 70 I am now studying the questions.

ROAD COMPANIONS

I would never have been able to make my journey to an over the hill place without my friends. I have been very lucky with cronies. Each of them supplied me with hiking poles for my climb upward. They are stimulating, generous and very, very witty. I value these people in and of themselves but most of all they could make me laugh out loud. There is nothing better for rehabilitating the body and spirit.

Evelyn's banter is the quickest draw in the West. She also listened in silence through the hard times without offering advice unless asked. She was at my wedding. She was at his funeral. For thirty years Evelyn and husband Dan were there at every hospital stay even when consciousness escaped me.

My friend Anita stocked my refrigerator and drove me home from more than one of my sick bays. Mark Twain would envy her humor. Her oral essays on the attending physicians were the miracle drugs. Her accountant husband Sy did a budget plan and signed a bank note until I could return to a work force. He is given to puns. Not my favorite brand of funny but thank goodness they are of an elegant variety.

During a convalescence from a lung surgery. Shirley came to my house every day at 6 a.m. to walk a block, then two, etc. until

I could walk alone. On one such visit, she staggered in with groceries and announced "Being wonderful is hard work."

Kathy and I share a particular sense of the ridiculous. We have wiped away a lot of tears of laughter through the decades. Although our lives are programmed so differently, sipping from the same cup of whimsy seals a unique bond of intimacy. She is both psychotherapist and a master gardener. We have much in common with the former and none with the latter. When she plants the flowers in pots on my balconies, she makes me promise I will speak gently to them. Every once in a while I announce to the floral arrangements "Kathy loves you." It is just enough heart for them to blossom but not flourish. Kathy replants my balcony every other year.

Some old cohorts have been around since before we grew permanent teeth. I appreciate my history with them. We remain interested in each other's comings and goings. We share an occasional holiday picnic and continue to play an infrequent game of bridge which requires only small talk.

But those who make up the bright threads in the fabric of my life know how to wring the zest from our "veil of tears." These special people who trudge upward bound with me share a unique sense of comedy. In between chuckles there are solemn philosophical dialogues and social commentaries about the meaning of life. Each of us offer our tilted view. In the final analysis, there may not be consensus. No matter. The excitement of discussion is primary. Although our bodies are shrinking some, we can grow taller as we climb that hill to aged.

I appreciate all my loving friends. But I am especially grateful for those who enjoy that nugget of zaniness. They are the ones who provide the sweetener as we squeeze the lemons for our lemonade.

THE ONES WE LOVE

My relatives are separated by moon miles. Those of us who do live in the same town are separated by interests. Others are scattered across the country. So since there is little contact with blood ties, I forged ties with strangers. They became the friends who make up the fabric of my life.

Still, a distant cousin's child calls me as he visits my city and I make an extra place at my dinner table that very night. I don't have to know a thing about this person. He is welcomed with affection. Someone I have never seen before wears the face of my father. Without any prior role in my life, he has an assigned title. He needs no permission to belong to my tribe.

Friends who are close to my heart have won a place there through long personal history and a host of mutual experiences. This newcomer paid no dues. Membership is automatic.

Blood connections are not inviolate however. I have no sacred obligation to love, respect or lend money to someone with whom I share an ancestry. I don't even have to like them. The one thing I can't do is deny them. To paraphrase Descartes "They exist therefore they are." Even my Aunt Sarah who can be a pain in the ear lobe.

Should Auntie ever become too frail to maintain her
independent living, some of us relatives just might consider inviting
her to live with them. If it was my weak moment, I would veto my
rash idea in a flash. That would not make me a villain. Far from it.
I acknowledge some obligation because she is blood related. She is
self-involved and petty but I could not completely abandon this less
than favorite relative.

Our concern for loving friends might be stronger and deeper
than for a family member. During a thorny patch, we respond to
each other as if we were kin. But no matter how devoted we are to
friends, we are not responsible in the same way. Friendship is a
privilege we earn and enjoy. Family members have a birthright.

Naturally, there are serious estrangement in every clan. No
allegiances are given, none expected. Common lineage is devalued.
Maybe properly so! Aaron Burr really embarrassed his father. John
Wilkes Booth all but ruined his brother's career. Aunt Sarah is just
an irritating bore.

Nonetheless, unless there is a radical rupture, one family
member usually ranks among the top ten important people in our
lives. Actually, that person would have been chosen for a good
friend anyhow.

A SMALL LUST FOR LEARNING

No one adored poor Van Gogh. He starved, cut off an ear and died without selling two paintings. Few recognized his genius. It took both the public and the pros nine decades to salute it.

The majority of art critics trashed Jackson Pollock. Viewers giggled. He ignored the ridicule and kept splashing his canvas. Surprise! Surprise! We realize now his work had deliberate intent. Technique unorthodox for the time but the patterns were structured. Today they hang in famous museums and wealthy houses.

Professional art experts have either agreed or disagreed with each other through the centuries. Occasionally they misjudged a trailblazer. Sometimes they championed mediocre performance. Yet for the most part, the critics know why an art object is or is not wonderful. I don't - ever. I wish I did.

My dear friend Elenore tells me I don't have to. She is an art historian who writes for important art periodicals and believes the uneducated audience need only feel. If our eyes and heart respond, we have enjoyed a creative experience. That opinion reassures my judgment. Yet, I am not fully convinced. Sentimental reactions could also reflect my ignorance.

It's not too late to add to my sorry store of information. I prefer to understand some of the details which mark real talent. My informed opinion will not automatically become right, but at least it won't be reduced to an illiterate "yuck."

History has demonstrated the staying power of the truly brilliant. I want to be able to recognize possible candidates for genius in my neighborhood. The old masters were once my age.

True, we don't need to be astronomers to appreciate the beauty of the stars. But knowledge does not destroy beauty. It merely adds to the wonder of it.

THE BALANCE SHEET

I am one of 8 million, 397 hundred thousand people in the United States over 60 years of age who live alone. 26% of us are childless. Whether we are alone by design or misfortune, there is no one in our lives to care for us out of legal or moral obligation.

Happily, I developed intimate relationships with auxiliary families. I am an honorary aunt to loving adults, a grandmother figure to their children. I am claimed as a relative by more than one family. Every holiday celebration brings several invitations. Somehow, I stitched together strong connections with people based on love and respect.

I launched an absorbing career in lieu of a home life. I had freedom to make decisions independently. Dollars went further for travel, clothes and health spas. Luxuries were soothing and I was solvent enough to buy a new car whenever I fancied one. I also tithed and volunteered to charities and community services.

According to the statistical projections from the National Institute of health, those millions of us over 60 years of age with no living relatives have at least 20 more years of a solitary life. Some of those years will be lived in isolation. On the other hand, of course, there must be millions of parents whose kids never visit. Life may not be fair but sometimes it evens out.

A PLACE TO TALK, LISTEN AND LEARN

My Aunt Sarah calls support groups "the huddled masses" or "havens for the helpless." It doesn't matter that she has neither participated nor does she understand the nature of these gatherings. She insists there would be no benefit for her to engage in any consortium devoted to miseries. "How could a headless group heal the crack in my crown"? she asks. She implies that people who complain in public forum are basically deficient. All Aunt Sarah has is a migraine condition untouched by potion yet prescribed for her. She sees no benefit to sharing this problem with strangers.

Her stance manages a rationale of sorts. She thinks there is something shabby about cheering ourselves up at the expense of our neighbors. It is her belief that one's own hunger pangs cannot be minimized because others are starving next door. In addition, the person with Parkinson's Disease or a manic-depressive husband cannot grasp the pain of her occasional disability?

My only experience with a support group is a generic one. I joined an Asthma organization to meet people who had what I had. There is little that is scarier than feeling singled out to suffer an infirmity alone. My support group's common concerns reassured me that Asthma was not visited on me by a personal demon. But that's not all. It was amazing how many practical suggestions my partners in pain had discovered to improve their days. There are

homely methods of easing symptoms or shortening convalescence.
We tell each other about new, inexpensive equipment, emergency
resources, and creative ways to add to our bank of hardier periods.
This kind of help is available from no one or nowhere else. Nifty
maneuvers my medical advisors never thought of or forgot to tell me.

Every disease or atypical condition has a support group
available. It's major purpose is to provide a brace to meet a life
straight on. This may require three meetings, a few months, the rest
of our natural lives. It takes just as long as it takes.

Meanwhile back at Aunt Sarah's. She was finally convinced
to attend a meeting of a Neurological Seminar devoted to
undiagnosed headaches. An announcement was made inviting
people to participate in a group meeting later that afternoon. She
went. While she still thinks an assembly of fellow sufferers are
"cripples incorporated who whine a lot", she has learned methods of
relief when attacks strike. She will never admit it but Aunt Sarah
has learned to lighten her load by sharing it.

A SKEIN OF GOLD

Society holds the notion that citizens shuffle off to old age at around sixty. No longer true. Statistically, we are now in the last third of our life-span when we reach 60. We only qualify as late middle-aged. Medical technology has replaced the last breath with a second wind. And with a little wisdom and a lot of luck these could be some of our best years. Harriet Doer's first book "Stones for Iberra" was a critical and commercial success when she turned seventy-two years old. Estelle Reiner, Carl's wife, and Rob's mother began a career as a jazz singer at 64.

Probably all of us wonder sometimes how our lives could have been different if we hadn't had obligations that limited our choice. Most of us are smart enough to harbor no regrets. Roads not taken could have led to swamp lands as well as glory.

But now folks, it is a whole new ball game. We have time for old dreams and new experiences. What a terrific unexpected bonus. It is also more than a little scary. It reminds me of my earlier adolescence when I could only fantasize about any choices because a depression family was dependent on sensible selections in order to survive the hard times. Like most of my schoolmates, I skipped higher education for the job that offered the most security. It was not important we like our tasks; it was vital we got paid for them. But at this new awkward age we get to dust off a few fantasies.

True we may have outgrown some of our early dreams. Maybe we no longer want to be teachers, firemen or FBI agents. But in case we do, there are ancillary but major roles in all those fields. The Retired Senior Volunteer Program is one organization in the business of filling holes in the community and fulfilling our latter years' fancies. We could even ask them about the circus that comes to town. They probably have all the high wire artists they need but there can never be too many clowns. And even the circus needs an accountant.

We are free to castle build. If we don't like the neighborhood, we move on. It has to be successful if for no other reason than we had the spirit to try. Of course, if you plan to invest the family fortune in yet another Pizza chain, it might be prudent to practice twirling a few somewhere before you put up the cash.

Longevity should be like a surprise party at midnight. A smorgasbord. We should sample anything we can digest. If we love it, we can come back for seconds.

THOU SHALT NOT DEFRAUD OR PLUNDER

I don't remember who said "We have the government we deserve." I know who said, "we have the goods and service we tolerate." I did!

We have come to accept shoddy merchandise and indifferent service as a way of life. Manufacturers bank on our tacit permission for that. Too many of us toss the ailing hair dryer or replace the young but very ill television set.

Must we remain helpless in the face of the Corporate Giant? Nope! To the contrary. The aging consumer is the jumbo market. Most of us have more spending cash than any other buying population. Corporations need to please us. So if the business community does not deliver quality merchandise with happy smiles, shame on them. If we allow them to discount the customer, shame on us.

There are several ways to effect change. Tantrums may be the least effective. Store managers will think us old cranks and cover the losses themselves. Secret vows never to buy x brand again won't work. Companies which spend millions on advertising and marketing strategies don't bankrupt or improve their stuff just because we pout in silence. When we make our dissatisfactions known to those in oval offices, attention will be paid. Firms are more guilty of incompetence than blatant fraud. The customer is most often short changed than cheated. The corporate world is probably eager to keep our good will. Public libraries list the Chairman of the Boards of companies. A personal letter will get to his desk. It need not be a hostile one. A clear statement of facts will do. Any established concern will respect a legitimate grievance.

I am relentless. Among the items apologetic moguls have replaced for me is a clock radio which didn't tell time or wake me up, a vaporizer, and a lawn mower. I have received rebates from airlines, rent-a-car establishments, and major cosmetic makers. To name a few. Newsweek answered my note notifying them of an offensive perfume ad. The president of the publishing company took the time to write a letter of apology with a promise that it would never happen again. Newsweek is my magazine above all others. Unless I experience flagrant rudeness, I do not complain about service to management. I deliver a direct speech to the offending representative. "What a pity you must make your living doing something you hate. It most be a torment to work with the public. You really should think about going into some other field." When I encounter gracious, sincerely helpful salespeople, a note of appreciation is sent to personnel or department heads.

Personal economics is not my prime motive for confrontation. Outrage is. I have little financial power but "they" may not caveat emptor on my head anyway. And as I demand better business standards, I hope to be speaking for all of us.

Asserting a consumer's right takes time and energy. If we are to return to the pride of workmanship and service, we must assume some active role. The responsibility to complain should be taken as seriously as the responsibility to vote. When we exercise our consumers rights we will get what we are entitled to. If we don't we will get what we got.

THE WAXED FRUIT SOCIETY

Welcome to the world of wrinkle free. It's nice for blouses but I am not sure about faces. My television screen is filled with old time movie stars with waxed apple expressions. I recognize only their voices which remain distinctive. Good thing. Other features are assembly lined.

Plastic surgery is a respectable bit of magic. Men and women are able to correct crippling disfigurements or nature's unattractive mistakes. But perhaps nature's most unattractive mistake is the lust for perfection. Now that it is possible to reshape ourselves, there are those who want it all. The physical anatomy can become man made. There are synthetic bits and pieces which can be added. Limbs lengthened or shortened to adjust our height. The surgeon giveth or taketh away. Take away is more popular.

There are compelling medical reasons for removal of certain body parts. Even fussy insurance companies will pay for those procedures. My niece had breast reductions in order to escape the intolerable abrasions caused by bra straps. One of the most powerful cases for increment surgery is the one following mastectomies. That operation reinstates a bearable image for some women who lose their breasts to cancer. And artificial joints allow once disabled limbs to move normally again.

Well, maybe cosmetic relief improves the lot of people who need it psychologically as well. In a nation where it is very good to look good, it is terrific if you look both good and young. A little painful snipping and bone cracking is worth it to some. Sara Jane had her face scraped to wipe away the wrinkles. Ann and her husband Sam had their eyes and chins "fixed" together and shared a hospital room. Those who can afford the expense, the misery, and the impermanence of an unpleated face have my support.

But I am not going to have my thighs sucked, my face lifted or reconstruction surgery. I am not sure I would submit to any more major operations let alone elective ones. Saying all that, I recently had a cataract from an eye removed. Hooray! It was about as inconvenient as having a tooth crowned and I can read again. Aren't current marvels of medical antidotes wonderful? Available sorcery for our personal nirvana.

THE FAMILY THAT NEVER WAS

More than a half century ago, the Saturday Evening Post featured a cover celebrating Thanksgiving. A perfect Grandpa carving a perfect turkey for a perfect family. Each face happy, and grateful. Norman Rockwell, the Poster King, had provided the American people a fable to live by. This glossy illustration became a personal ideal for people throughout the nation.

Lord knows, Thanksgiving togetherness was a sacred goal in my house. Come meetings of our clan, we tried our best to appear flawless. We never even came close. Oh sure, there were armed truces for the occasion. Relatives who hadn't spoken to one another since the last mandatory gathering wore frozen party smiles. Year after year, we girded our loins and continued to attend those compulsory dinners. Occasionally resolve paid off. There were a few years when a terrific menu and mellow wine made the event almost pleasant.

Pleasant is terrific for most families. Yes, there are those within a bloodline who genuinely like each other and who socialize with no agenda. The rest of us are merely linked by genealogy. It is a pull comparable to the law of gravity. Obligations assigned at birth are almost impossible to ignore.

Probably nowhere is the Norman Rockwell ideal of a family dinner reproduced. Not even at Norman's. He painted a fantasy from a photograph. A pictorial composition arranged with strangers from one another. Literally. Prototypes hired from a modeling agency in July for that year's November issue. Grandpa came from Hollywood casting.

It is foolish to worship a fraudulent scene. In an era when family values are in question, we are engaged in a struggle to determine which tribal traditions are merely habit and which are sacred. Surely, there are enough genuine rites to preserve in a contemporary society.

We often romanticize the bygone agrarian society as the idyllic family past. More likely they were bound by economic dependence. Children were necessary farm hands. Adult males remained on the farm more from the promise of profit than loyalty. Ultimately they would inherit the land.

When sons married, their families were housed in or around the old homestead. Wives were melded into a domestic work force which produced the daily essentials. Unmarried daughters with almost no opportunities for paid employment were blended into the family structure and forced to assume bothersome tasks for which they were repaid with life long security.

All this togetherness fostered the illusion that those years were rich with devotion. Not necessarily so. Hostility and resentment often flourished among people trapped into situations of no choice. Sibling rivalry was often bitter. Those family ties could be handcuffs.

The Industrial Revolution set them free and into motion. Motorized vehicles made manpower less important at The House on the Prairie. So when tractors and milking machines released the young, they flocked to cities finding new sources of income. No longer totally dependent upon Papa's legacy, progeny could now survive on their own if needs be; fusion was no longer mandatory.

But human creatures are born into a unit; a fixed network which feeds, houses and protects the young until they are tall enough to fend for themselves. This evolution makes for a durable connection. Separation through distance and life-styles does not diminish our need for that unique human warmth. Visits back home resemble the quest for a Holy Grail. Too Bad! It does not rest on that mantel piece.

BEWARE OF THE TIME BANDIT

Having passed my age of majority a few times over, I feel entitled to abandon the hustle. Overload being no longer a way of life, my agenda holds two categories: amusement and necessity. The list of essentials is short. My body must be kept clean and sound. End of list.

The Amusement Inventory is longer. It is also varied. Bridge, theater and swimming and traveling are on my fun list. My cousin who is an ardent gardener happily toils among his plants from dawn to dusk. Only a chain gang could motivate such a project for those who adore shopping, or competition chess. Some of us armchair participants may want to sample all of it at the movies.

It's all fair. The punch clock says "vacation with pay." Whatever number of days remain on that sun dial belong to me. I am free to spend them in whatever splendor I can muster. "Shoulds, and must dos" that still appear on my daily duty roster are evaluated carefully. I eliminate and reshuffle what I can. I am primed for maximum diversion.

Why then, now that I own all my days do they zip by without frolic? Why is there still that litany of vital, icky errands? Who or what is stealing my golden moments?

In an effort to understand the mystery, I telephoned a friend to remind me of the scientific method formula to find a solution. According to Bill's definition of scientific method, I approached my dilemma clinically. (1) The problem - Time Leakage. (2) The hypothesis - I believe unfettered persons are able to bask endlessly in leisurely pursuits. (3) Method of collecting data - I documented my every action for one week.

What a shock. I get mail every day but Sunday. All of it gets read because I once tossed a check which looked like junk. And I spend a lot of time eating. An unhurried repast with friends instead of running around with a sandwich while doing chores during a lunch hour. I also take a full hour to dine alone while watching a TV rerun that had escaped me during my busy years. And if one eats, one must grocery shop. Nowadays, it is not critical to wheel Olympic style through the supermarket aisles with an iron clad buying plan. I saunter, menu planning as I go. I can't believe this once twenty minute errand now bloats to an afternoon outing.

The week that I examined my comings and goings included a trip to the dentist, the hairdressers, the cleaners, and the drugstore. My editor called twice because my rewrites were late. Oh yes, I have to factor in my new career. Silly me, I thought writing would be on my amusement list between luncheon engagements. Instead it now appears on my necessity side of the ledger in large print.

My time study indicates that my hypothesis was faulty. Tempus simply fugits at the same rate it ever did. It's my attitude that needs reality adjusting. I am disappointed when I am scheduled with appointments two days in a row. However, my desire for an unhasty life and the drive to enjoy companionship are at war with my drive to leave behind a written record.

I must remind myself that no one can govern moments by whim or by golly. My entertainment inventory needs to be revised. The authority to set priorities is mine and it is I who feel compelled to impose some value judgment. I promise myself that an hour won't be squandered on a five minute task just because I can claim 60 minutes to do it. I further make a vow not to berate myself should covenants be bent a little and I suck my thumb a morning or two. In the final analysis, I want to savor these years but satisfactions that come with continued growth are not found in the freedom of an unintended life.

THE "IF ONLY" FICTION

My family put great store in being rich, pretty and thin. That combination was supposed to insure the supreme American Dream. Some of us suspected cause and effect didn't work like that. I never thought those born with a silver spoon had an automatic tool to paradise. It merely provides comfort. Beauty alone guarantees nothing but good looks. Reducing diets meant less of us and not more of anything else. We read of famous lovelies whose despair was fatal.

Yet the fantasy persists that lives would be perfect if we had some lucky advantage like money and looks. We cannot seem to curb the appetite for windfalls. It has been known to happen about as often as snow in the tropics.

Yet, the majority of us accomplish our goals without special advantages and lots of effort. Education is a sound investment. Formal or otherwise. The more rounded the better. While that doesn't provide a warranty for those missing pieces we are born without, it helps. Deficiencies compensated by experience and hard work.

There are some old adages that hold up. Money and looks don't hurt is one. The search and seizure of financial security is very rewarding if one does not expect nirvana. The cliche "pretty is as pretty does", however, misses the mark by a mile too. Good deeds do not beautify. Comely requires a little smarts to make it count. My Fair Lady had to learn to talk and walk fine enough to give her looks importance.

My own needs are modest. Enough cash to help the homeless. Adequate funds to feed a few elegant hobbies.

Still, I would also like to be rich, slim and stunning. Tough. Like Popeye, "I 'yam what I' yam."

GROWING UP BEFORE GROWING OLD

Signposts toward adulthood used to be clear. Events such as a driver's license, an electric shaver, a pair of nylons or a school graduation, were once markers. The significance of these moments have become fuzzy. Certainly, sweet sixteen has lost its earlier magic. Kindergartners wear cap and gown and the faces of preteens imitate a world weary sophistication. Important milestones have been diluted.

The United States government has decided that 18 year olds are full grown. They may vote and fight wars. Unfortunately not many do the former and too many do the latter. And although they are not of legal age in a liquor store, alcoholism is common among our youth.

Those of us deep in our majority claim we would be young again only under one condition: we would have to know then what we know now. Well what is it we know now? Do we really understand the concept of "responsibility precedes revenue"? Always? Was it just rotten kids who poisoned our shell fish? Certainly it could not be older corporation heads or political figures educated in our best universities playing Russian Roulette with our public health.

How about the one acid-test of maturity which meant taking consequences for our actions? Are all our junk-bond dealers under

13 years of age? Where did they learn to mishandle our social/
economic structure? A public trust is a sacred trust. Or at least a
lawful one. When an occasional administrator of a charitable
organization or university embezzles or misappropriates funds for
personal gain, our confidence in philanthropy is shaken. Shame on all
those big children in grown-up clothes who flunked the entrance
exam to citizenship.

It's not only the Americans who are parading as rational,
full-grown human beings. All over the world there are men and
women racing toward their allotted four-score-ten having baby
tantrums. Severe enough to threaten the world.

Folklore once had it that wisdom was the province of the
elders. Their hope was the strength of the generation following
them. But our modern middle-age juveniles seem to skip the search
for knowledge which would include ethics. They need just enough
information to hack a path to fame and fortune. Shows how much
we have learned in the five and a half thousand years we have been
walking around on our hind legs.

My Uncle Ben was fond of saying, "Too Old Schmart". I
think he meant, too late schmart. But he never lost his faith. Uncle
Ben continued to vote even when his heroes were tarnished. He
continued to care. He was convinced that people would survive and
overcome. Over and over until they got it right.

DETOURS

"I grow old, I grow old. I wear my trousers rolled.... Dare I eat a peach?" moaned the immortal poet T.S. Eliot when he was only 29 years of age. And he spent almost half a century dreading the day he might be forced to gum his food.

Troubadours have always railed against the length of human seasons. They express our rage and our fear because if the time is short, it's unfair. If the inevitable end of life is full in measure, the waiting room is uncomfortable. Shakespeare wrote of the "mewling years."

I want to pay homage to the ways the human spirit can renew itself. Some of us survive nature's disasters with enormous spirit. In her 65th year, my friend Diana lost most of her sight with no warning. She awoke one day to find her world suddenly dark. Her kinship to that world was bound by her scholarship. It remains so. The Braille Institute recordings have made it possible for her to keep current with the new crop of authors and to revisit the masters.

Diana was not born or bred to sport a sunny disposition. She does not believe in karma or destiny. What Diana has faith in is facts. She is near blind. And while Diana is not without some bitterness, it is not enough to defeat her. She takes advantage of all the equipment designed for poor-vision people. She has even discovered a few helping techniques of her own.

My friend Carolyn who was born and bred to have a sunny disposition had a mastectomy 20 years ago. She accepted the bare spot on her chest calmly and was relieved the cancer was gone with her breast. The day after surgery, she hurried down the hospital corridor to a scale. She was seriously disappointed her weight hadn't changed. "How much does a breast weigh?", she asked the nurses at the work station nearby.

I grieve for people like T.S. who shiver through the summer of their lives anticipating winter. We forgive Eliot because he was a creative genius and his laments were couched in immortal verse. Common folk without his gifts are just an ordinary pain. To themselves, their families, or to anyone in earshot of their perpetual melancholy about the hangnails of life. They might be lonely as well as irritating. I wouldn't invite a chronic complainer to my Thanksgiving table.

We ought to be able to enjoy the cherries before we get to the pits. It makes sense to invest in health insurance, storm windows, and to patch the roof before the rains come.

Once the basics are in place, I would not want to devote my years preparing for calamities. Most don't happen anyhow. In the meantime, I don't want to miss a dance, a laugh or dessert.

BEWARE OF TROJAN HORSES

I rarely give a practical gift to newlyweds. Essentials may be their first priority but, excluding the truly poverty stricken, one can always manage to get necessities. It's those nominal luxuries like a vase or a wine cooler that are usually neglected. Placed on a list for later on, they rarely move to priority status. I like to provide that little bit of gourmet jam that belongs on anybody's staff of life.

Gift giving is an art. Like all art, it has a few basic rules. First and foremost, it must be an item that would excite the recipient. Marion would love to be sitting first row center at a Rolling Stone Concert to celebrate her birthday. She would rather be sitting there with Donald than with me. So I provide two tickets for her and him at a cozy celebration lunch for the two of us.

Gifts shouldn't ever disguise a critique. A lady bountiful friend once replaced a necklace of mine with one far more expensive and of superior quality. She told me that I was better than that awful mediocre gold necklace I had been wearing. I didn't consider it a present. I thought it was a cruel bit of criticism. It might have aggrandized the giver but it made me feel like Little Orphan Annie.

I love to give and get presents. It is not a problem for me when affluent friends give me extravagant booty. I make no effort to duplicate in kind but try to reciprocate with something special chosen with care. A classic record album difficult to come by or a modest novelty item that will make them smile. And occasionally an article beyond my means because I find something so "them."

My friend Evie has a gift shelf. It has items on it that people have given her for which she has no use. It does come in handy for those days she is invited to a dinner party and has no time to shop for the required wine or flower. Voila! The very thing appears from her shelf.

A stash of bridge score pads, a paperback mystery, or a small box of stationery for the right people makes Evie especially thoughtful. Which she is!

My friend Bob was given a very ugly wallet from his friend Stan on his 50th birthday. Bob gave this wallet to Frank on his birthday. Eventually, this wallet make its way back to Stan for one of his birthdays. Stan returned it to Bob for his 55th birthday. It had made the complete rounds among close pals. A treasured tradition. A newcomer to the group knows he has earned his place in the intimate circle when he gets the wallet.

Accompanying couples of my generation to dinner can be a sensitive matter. Some husbands feel it is their role to pay the check. I understand their discomfort about sharing the cost and allow them to pay for us all but I am emancipated enough to feel slightly insulted. So as a result we seldom dine out together and I feel obligated to reciprocate with theater tickets which are more expensive then my share of dinners. The more liberated husbands among us permit me to pay my share and we dine out together often.

There is no equality in gift giving nor should there be. The friendship bank is not an investment that pays dividends in goods. It's the intangible we exchange that is the most meaningful.

FOLD THAT UMBRELLA -
THE SUN IS OUT

Those of us who have lived through the Great Depression of the Thirties will always remember the experience. It is indelible. We worked hard for small pay and were thrilled at the opportunity. Just to survive those years was a victory.

The basic economic rule of that era was very simple. When we spent it, we did not have any more. Some learned good fiscal habits to insure their financial security. Others will never feel financially secure again no matter what.

Money management books and seminars specializing in the Senior Citizen have become very popular. Good thing too. Everyone should know how to make the most from their income. But perhaps we also need some workshops on How to Spend.

Depression children in their latter years do not always permit themselves affordable luxuries. We've become victims of thrift even when we no longer need to.

My very solvent friend Marilyn has an extra gentle cycle on her washing machine yet she hand washes her underpants to prolong their life. Her underpants will outlive her. Clarice boasts that she buys only secondhand clothes and day-old bread. She considers it wasteful to spend even a teeny sum to buy sheer pleasure or freedom from a drudgery. Any surplus of cash after necessary expenses is saved for a rainy day. Well, for some of us it has begun to drizzle. If we ever plan to enjoy some pricey occasions, now is the time to do it.

A large percentage of the young are living with big mortgages, unpaid-for automobiles and we worry for them. Understandable. People from the bad times do not understand living in comfort on the bank's borrowed money. The young among us simply do not believe in deferred living. They have a sense of entitlement never before known to the common person. Yes, many of them will lose their unpaid for elegance during a serious recession. Many more will find a way to protect their standard of living through new business ventures and second careers. Engineers pried from executive offices are opening hardware stores and studying computer programming. This younger generation is able to work hard and with more confidence than the one preceding theirs. They know how awful it is to be poor. Their Depression era grandparents have told them often enough.

It is painful to need things we cannot afford.

Another misfortune, however, is the inability to spend for fear of poverty. Chances to finally indulge ourselves are not infinite. I am not talking major league. But if the cost of a box of out-of-season strawberries, a concert or a candlelight dinner will not pauperize us, let's do it. We have gathered our Rose Buds. Let's enjoy the fragrance.

WHO'S CRANKY?

Everyone alive has ploughed through a trauma or two. Somehow we live through them. But in my experience, it is the pimples in life which are lethal. Rashes differ from local to local. I find, for instance, that Country roads holding more than three cars are considered a traffic problem by the same people who will wait patiently for one lone waitress to serve a room of fifty. City folk willingly contend with grid lock but expect a warm-up before the second cup of coffee.

Older citizens are often thought of as testy. No WE are not. I am. When that automatic "Have a nice day" tic comes from the grocery checker, the pharmacist, the car mechanic, and every sales person I encounter within 24 hours, it ruins any hope of my having one.

Surely Department Store employees should know the route to the restrooms. "Over there" is not a very specific direction. My bladder has been in trouble more than once by vague instructions. When one encounters those who are genuinely helpful, it is hard not to grovel in gratitude.

The collapse of things which are supposed to improve my life also makes me stamp my foot. My VCR develops a virus two days after the warranty expires. My toaster oven doesn't toast or bake and needs returning. Then there are spray cans which lose their hiss at time of purchase. Hard to believe they are effective enough to pollute our skies. They must have an evil manufacturing partner. A pox on the cans and all who make them.

No point in complaining about things to airplane companies. My first flight to Europe was delayed long enough so that friends waved bon-voyage as I left on a bus for a hotel until we could be airborne. When we were finally aloft, we were treated to a chicken dinner which had a life of its own.

If any reader understands their telephone bill, please let me know. You are not obligated to explain it to me. Just reassure me that it is not a secret between androids.

And then there are the numbers game. When I memorized my address and telephone number, my driver's license, the numerals on my social security card, I figured that was enough to tax my memory. I never imagined that this task would multiply by zip codes, ten digit phone numbers, a fax machine and a battalion of charge cards. A slip of an integrator on any one of these identification items and we are doomed to bad credit purgatory. My bank assigned my deposits to another on the strength of one introverted digit.

Am I a pompous grouch? Maybe but I don't think social hives are the exclusive product of the 2oth century. Ancient kings also suffered from boils of irritation. They sought relief by banishing any fool who blighted their day. Common folk like me just gnash their teeth to the gum line.

SCENT SENSE

Millions among us remember or heard about how families used a galvanized bath tub every Saturday night. It was such a huge production that frequent bathing was regarded as unhealthy.

Today we know better. The daily ritual of cleansing our bodies is good for us. Purists use refreshing unscented soaps and deodorants. Others don't. They douse themselves with fragrant bath powders, perfumes, hair sprays and shaving lotions. It's an ancient tradition.

When Queen Elizabeth needed a bath, her hand-maidens sprinkled scented water on her royal person. Cleopatra was famous for her aromatic oils and lotions. Beau Brummel's wigs smelled heavily of incense. These style-setters were creative in the big cover-up of the day.

What stench do we need to disguise in the 1990s? Almost everyone has at least one room devoted to modern plumbing. We emerge after a regular scrub naturally fresh. Yet many still pour enough lotions to resemble a walking flower garden. A fake bit of nature that would choke a bumble bee.

Why? One reason is that as one ages the sense of smell loses its former keenness. But the lungs know what the nose does not.

Strong chemicals make strong odors. When you splash new and spicier products on your body, your bathroom walls or your laundry, you create a private pollution which invades all of us who stand in that immediate environment. Worse! Our ozone layer is crumbling from the action of all those aerosol cans. Now that stinks.

ON THE YELLOW BRICK ROAD

Some of us retired folk are moving our body parts all over the world. Many for the first time. There are those whose main passion is planning the trip. For them, learning about the destination through books and slides is half the fun. They plan and follow an itinerary taking full advantage of specific areas. These are your organized travelers.

Then there are mavericks like me who just like to wander. The programmers think of us as a careless lot lacking in both aesthetics and common sense. Not necessarily so. Some of the most exciting moments can be the result of happenstance. A sudden shower or an untimely heat spell sends us lurching into an unknown museum. It's more than a shelter. It's a find. A small exhibit by a soon-to-be well known artist or a yet unheralded collection by a very famous one.

Once I discovered a private Da Vinci showing of anatomical drawings in a London gallery almost free of tourists. I sauntered along savoring the event with only a guard who was so happy to see a human face, he offered to share his tea. Several years later these same pieces were assembled for a tour of major American cities. Lines of waiting crowds lined blocks to gain admittance to this exhibit.

Serendipity is not the province of the unplanned promenader. The unexpected happens to the carefully planned traveler as well. They take full advantage. A prior appointment, however, can spoil the full experience of an unforeseen delight. If one discovers an organ rehearsal while visiting the Notre Dame Cathedral in Paris but there is an arranged bus waiting to take one to the Palace at Versaille, then too bad. Only the languid can remain for the chance Bach concert.

Planners are fully aware that no matter how much details get arranged in advance, stuff simply happens. Schedules cannot be cast in concrete. The best of itineraries can be attacked by a weather tantrum delaying planes and missing hotel accommodations. Seasoned travelers are prepared for the truly unpredictable. Emergencies are dealt with incredible competence. Secondary blueprints are included as part of an "if needs be" formula. But they usually hate it.

Those who enjoy aimless ventures love it. They are rarely stranded without bed and bath. It is true that sleep over places might cost more money than they would like to spend. Or the unreserved spots might be plainer than hoped for. Grungy even. The cavalier wayfarer knows there will be bumps in an unfamiliar road. That's OK. A trade-off for the possibility of a chance adventure. There is no appointment book. They can prolong an occasion for a week or more - or else leave in the morning.

Once upon a time I made haste to visit the Canterbury Cathedral the day before I departed the British Isles. It was a Sunday and I caught a late morning train from London. When I asked the taxi driver to deliver me to the Abbey, he took me to a carefully preserved ancient dig preceding any Arch Bishop of Canterbury. It was an open air affair and once more I had the complete attention of the guards on duty who escorted me to every mound explaining details not found in any brochure. It was a thrilling accident.

The Canterbury Cathedral museum closed five minutes after my arrival. But another ironic blessing. There is an operative albeit modest cathedral at Canterbury. It is attended by the towns people for miles around. Sabbath Services were about to begin. The sermon that Sunday was about the American phenomenon which took place that week. The landing on the Moon. Another exhilarating day for a dislocated traveler.

I admire those orderly globe trotters who can diagram the most exotic trip for maximum experiences. They even allot elbow room for random pleasure. I resent only their arrogance. They recommend which hotel, what to do and where to dine before departure. Upon return they sometimes devalue my choices, puzzled by my carelessness and miffed because I ignored their advice. How could I have dismissed their hard work of research with such perfect results? They may never understand the special excitement for that spontaneous soul who packs the luggage with no iron clad route in mind.

There is enormous contrast between "free spirits." Some are frankly impulsive. I know people like that. Definitive plans are a prison sentence. They want what they want - right now. They are propelled into action without weighing outcome. Charge cards were invented for them.

On the other hand spontaneous people pay their bills before they leave and arrange for plants to be watered during their absence. The exact return date may not be known but they are prepared to assume a structured life upon return. In the meantime the only plan is to have no plan. A vacation from the list of things to do.

Spontaneity is a rehearsal for old age. No one can have a map for this adventure. We can only try for the best. Some of us get very lucky along the way. Bones and organs remain hale and hearty. Others exercise perfect health routines only to be scuttled by a gene pool. The adaptable among us will manage with whatever happens. All the way into three digits birthdays. Or at least that is the plan.

THINGS THAT GO BOO IN THE NIGHT

I have had a goodly share of dreadful experiences.
Earthquakes, floods, fire and poverty have not escaped me. As I
gather resources to salvage the salvageable with as little angst as
possible, there are those who call me "Little Mary Sunshine" or
"Rebecca of Sunny Brook Farm". I don't think so. Hair pulling and
chest beating hurts. Why add to pain?

It's not as though I don't acknowledge losses. Hard not to
notice when several of my body parts were removed. I don't miss
my breasts as much as that lung lobe but once I said "Oh Shit" a few
dozen times, what else to do but go on with the equipment left
behind.

Conversely, there are friends who glorify my efforts to
persevere. I don't know if all that applause is deserved.   I am one
of those lucky people who can accept what is beyond my control. I
don't like it but I bear it. Some of us hate loss of control more than
the event itself.

Oft-times whatever seemed like bravery were knee jerk
reactions to endure whatever fell in my path. I will, however, take
credit for deliberate decisions.

I do battle with those things over which I have power. I shall not be afraid to buy seats at the symphony, theater or ballet because of their location rather than cost despite a limited income. I pay professionals to wash my car and clean my stove. Should the wherewithal run out before I do, I'll pay the consequences.

KITTENS ARE CUTE

I suffer from nausea when younger people use terms such as sweet or dear to describe the older citizen. Especially when the adjectives are preceded by little. Little ole people I know would use all their little ole bulk and swing their little ole purses at the well-meaning klutz who thinks aging is darling, sweet or dear. We who have shrunk, who squint or shuffle with age don't feel adorable.

The young cannot possibly know what it is like to be old any more than I can really comprehend what it is like to be an African American, a member of the 400, or a movie star. Reading about them gives me information which might allow me to understand the circumstances of their life better, but ultimately I have not walked in those moccasins.

No matter how much insight I might have gained on what it means to be black, rich, or famous from my friends who are among that slice of America, I cannot know that experience. Even the same experiences vary. There is no formula for how like backgrounds produce different individuals. I still remember the Warner Brothers movies of the 30's about brothers raised in the ghetto. Brother James Cagney was the gangster and sibling Pat O'Brien was the priest.

No matter from whence we older citizens came from, we

did not plan to become cute. The best of us sustain a penalty or two for reaching old. Worn-out bones ache and break, sounds become muffled and our immune system can no longer stand guard against viral winds. Aging is "like a box of chocolates" but we meet it with spirit and pluck. Not many of us ask to be pampered or stroked like a house pet.

PASSAGE

Few things in life are tougher than babyhood. Eyes don't focus and everything eaten turns to gas. Crying is the only form of communication and it takes a while for the big people to know the complaint. Is it hunger? A pat on the back for that extra burp? Does a diaper need changing? Again?

It gets better. The infant finds the first bit of autonomy when his fingers become a personal pacifier. Adults learn to know their baby's body language and can decipher the grunts for specific needs.

Babies, on the other hand, discover more in the first 12 months than a Ph.D. earned at Harvard. They learn to chew, crawl, stand, walk and run. They can identify Mama, Daddy, Aunts, Uncles, and Grandparents. Later, as toddlers, they will call them by names which are taught or invented. But no matter how precocious, dependence upon loving caretakers for food, clothing and shelter continues for several years before the human being child can forage for itself.

Poets in love with melodrama liken the physical decline of aging with the plight of the infant. Shakespeare for one called the very old "mewling as an infant." Not necessarily! While our internal organs may quarrel with each other on occasion and our sense of touch, sight, sound and smell could diminish more or less, it is only a real physical illness which will render us defenseless. Anytime I am tempted to mourn my declining mobility at 70, I remember the helplessness of an infant and I am glad for my independence. At the very least I can drive a car and sign a check.

EENNY MEENY MINEY MO

There was a time when there were only two kinds of cereals? One hot and one cold. The modern world has now produced a plethora of breakfast foods. An entire length on a supermarket aisle.

Dozens of staples in our world have been similarly multiplied. We are no longer limited to garden variety fruits and vegetables. Hot House farmers and world wide shippers offer us an infinite assortment. Horticulturists design brand new ones. Nectarines were one of the first and have been around so long we forget they were invented. I recently bought Asian bok choy and Finnish potatoes while traveling through a remote rural town in Oregon.

My interest in exploring new and improved does not extend to hardware. I find choices in equipment crazy-making. I do not want to compare and contrast the data for the dozens of different models of clocks, radios, and television sets. I want a gizmo that says "on." I want a gizmo that says "off."

When it comes to important once-in-a-great-while purchases, I remain absolutely loyal. I ignore the horde of new-make autos since our last purchase. My Toyota has been faithful and trouble-free and so I will buy the newer model of my old car if needs be. The burden of selection is simply too tough. Familiar is comfortable.

MYTH BUSTING

Sometime in recent history, the urban dweller became known as the "city slicker." The implication being that people who lived in metropolitan areas were cunning in ways unknown to honorable country folk. City sophisticates were no less judgmental. Rural residents were dubbed "rubes" not capable of understanding or dealing with complex life-styles. Not entirely true!

Fact is that Ma and Pa Kettle or the Beverly Hills Hillbillies are satire. I know a few bucolic types who are apt to whistle Mozart around the farm, and cultural centers in London or Rome do not fill each seat at their concert halls.

It seems stranger than fiction but lost wallets are returned to owners in big, bad cities. I know. I lost one in a taxi in Chicago last week. The driver who returned it to the hotel desk at 3 A.M. didn't seem to expect a reward. Not uncommon I am told.

Although stereotypes often escape reality, we are devoted to them. We discount the passion for gardening in the elegance of New York City. Poet Laureates mostly spring from plain places. Robert Frost and Carl Sandburg came to town for ceremonial doings like presidential inaugurations and returned quickly to their pastoral well spring.

Opera Houses and Art Galleries usually do not grow in suburbia. World Series games don't play there either. That's OK. with our rustic cousins. It's a fair trade-off. Those who yearn for culture and big-league ball games find ways to satisfy it with video and television. Occasionally they brave contamination of industrial smoke, smog and congestion to attend a Super Bowl or to hear live musicians in celebrated halls of sound and splendor. They know that there are times when television or high fidelity equipment cannot quite capture the excitement.

Then too, there are genuine nature lovers who live among skyscrapers. Picnics in the local park just don't do it. Vacations are spent in remote and wooded places where rural folk enjoy the trees, lakes and birds all year round.

How wonderful to visit all those places we wouldn't want to call home. Our design for life isn't necessarily superior. It is just ours. We don't need to deprecate others to elevate the station in which we live. We lucky ones who enjoy our chosen habitat can honestly say "there are nice people everywhere."

SECOND CHANCES

Dr. Oliver Sacks, the noted Neurologist, describes the case of a frantic patient who sustained a blow to his head which rendered him functionally blind. Dr. Sacks attempted an experimental procedure which restored the patient's normal vision in black and white. The man was a painter.

Time went by and the world of Neurology developed a new surgical technique which promised the return of color. Dr. Sacks was thrilled for the artist. He contacted his former patient and offered him the possibility of performing this operation. To the amazement of all, the artist refused the surgery. It seems that while he was deprived of color, he had perfected his art in stark black and white. He found this new art form so compelling he was afraid to contaminate it with color.

I love this story. Whenever I witness creative solutions to what appear to be impossible situations, it gives me hope for the planet. We will find a way to do what can't be done. We will uncover the mysteries of space, we will find harmless ways to dispose of our trash, limit crime, and cure AIDS. Tenacious and enterprising souls will keep shoveling the world's pile of manure hoping to find a pony.

SHORT SHRIFT

Recently, I was asked to give a talk to a Senior Citizen service group. I am usually a very good speaker, but last week I laid a big enough egg to make an omelet for fifty.

It is important to examine disasters. That exercise makes future success more reliable. Of course, there is no fail-safe formula for smash hits. Ask Phil Donahue, Oprah Winfrey, or David Letterman.

So what happened to me that day? Let's assume that the program was planned to accommodate a guest speaker. That the audience was primed and eager to hear my remarks. That the room was arranged to the best physical advantage. Even if not, I am too experienced a speaker not to accommodate to circumstances.

When I am engaged by professional groups, my preparation is very thorough. There is an enormous amount of advance planning. I make sure the concerns of the audience is known to me. Their needs determine the agenda. If a University or College request that I conduct a workshop, the seminar description will attract only those already interested in my topic. There will always be time set aside at the end of the day for questions and answers. There are written evaluations for me and the sponsoring institution to assess the presentation and content.

Normally there is a fee for my appearances. I make exceptions for a service group. It is flattering when they request my participation. I am also pleased to play a role in the community. So far so good. I took my responsibility seriously that day. Or did I?

I must admit I made no particular preparations for this group. I didn't think it was necessary for a fifteen minute talk. I lifted a portion from a hundred other speeches which would be appropriate to this occasion. I was convinced of conquest. Well, I came, I saw, I bombed.

It was truly a learning experience for me. For years I had told audiences that Senior Citizens differ from one another. Well, this particular group differed a lot from any I had ever faced before. They did not want to hear about the joys and challenge of aging as I enthusiastically endorsed the later years.

There is a faint cry of guilt. Could it be possible that I did not take my task seriously enough because it was a free engagement? I wouldn't like to think so. Other gratis talks had been triumphs.

The major problem was that they didn't want to hear about aging. It should have been my business to find out what they wanted to know before I told them what I knew. The next time I am asked to be a luncheon speaker before an unfamiliar assembly, I will prepare for it. I am too old for flop sweat!

THE WORN OUT BATTLE

Men and Women are different from each other. Everyone knows that. Most of us celebrate the contrast. All of us make a big fuss about the dissimilarities.

Linguistic specialist, Dr. Deborah Tannen has written a scholarly treatise on communication differences between the genders. Given parallel chairs in a room, 8 year old boys will remain seated side by side as they talk to each other. In the same situation, 8 year old girls will move the chairs to form a circle so that they can make eye contact with one another. It is a well-documented book in recent academic studies but it would seem old news to those in my generation. We have long noted the different verbal cues among the genders.

My male colleagues were praised for their straightforward directness. The female counterparts were declared arrogant. The men who could make hard decisions were called talented executives. Women were called something else altogether. And so on.

One of the strangest incidents in my career was at a medical conference. My woman boss was the Key Note Speaker. Although not a physician, she was a powerhouse in the health education field with a national reputation.

The local American Medical Association had assigned a young Oncologist to escort us during our two-day stay. There were newspaper and television interviews as well as a radio call-in show.

At the culminating conference dinner, there was a long dais where my Executive Director sat with the regional dignitaries. I was placed at one of the front round tables which seated ten people. The young, attractive physician sat next to me. He was occupied in conversation with an acquaintance on the other side of him when he suddenly turned to me and asked with some heat, "Ma'am, do you consider yourself a woman or a lady?" When I recovered from what sounded like an assault, I told him my understanding was that the classification of woman reflected an anatomical reality. And so I was sure that I was a woman. Since the term "lady" was a value judgment, that was open to interpretation. I never got a chance to ask why he asked. The program began. My boss was being introduced to the medical audience. After her introduction she adjusted her microphone saying "sometimes we forget what a little lady I am." She knew that this audience would accept her expertise seriously but would like her better if she admitted she was a only a little lady among male medical giants.

In an ageist society both sexes bear the brunt of unfair name calling. For instance an irreverent young girl is affectionately judged saucy. A defiant young man is spirited. The older citizen is a grouch. Middle-aged careerists are called persistent, much admired for their tenacity. When the aging persevere they are seen as stubborn and rigid. The young Beau Brummel becomes a dirty old man. The older woman still interested in a tryst or two is considered a nut case.

Earlier female pioneers in business, science and letters were more often patronized than admired but their modern heirs are building muscle as they climb the ladder of excellence. Still - mute and cute gets better service at the hardware store.

Senior Citizens carry with them the gender bias's of their youth. We call the overweight man portly. We call the plump woman fat.

The term old bachelor seems to have the wink of roué. Spinsters are obvious failures. And so on.

Understanding what we say and why we say it is really important. There is no form of bigotry worse than name-calling. Ignorant when it is unconscious. Ugly when it is deliberate. It is good to face some unalterable facts. Men and women are not alike. Vive La Difference. Old is not young. Thank goodness. I wish we did not have to criticize each other to illustrate the distinctions.

THE TICS OF THE CLOCK

As our children grow tall enough to reach the water tap, they gain a measure of independence. By the time they reach their legal majority, we are no longer accountable for them. Seems fair since they don't have to account to us either. We knew that would happen one day. Lifelong habits, however, are hard to break.

It seems natural for parents to be the ultimate judges. We have always done it. We may not have known how to do trigonometry but the report card wasn't official until we signed it. Now our adult offspring enter worlds alien to us and strangers sign their checks when they make the grade.

Their life experiences can be broader than ours as well. How can we warn a physician daughter she will catch cold if she takes off her sweater? We may not remind our minister son to be a good boy! We feel bereft because our advice and consent is no longer central to their lives.

Well now, hold on. We do have an important role. Trust me. It will be terrific. More power than an allowance. We will establish a mature friendship with our children. Caring friends give and receive advice from each other all the time, don't they? We use tact and discretion with peers. Friends don't get sent to their room when they get testy.

And if our opinions or suggestions come off as edicts, long friendships could end. Our children can be alienated too. Yet a divorce is rare among people related to each other by blood and/or memories.

Well, we may have to both compromise a bit. Mutual respect has a nice ring to it. When our children discover our once infallible wisdom has holes that a large truck could drive through, it will be a shock. With any luck at all they will also notice undiscovered qualities which will delight them. We may loathe what they do and how they do it but will try to pass no judgment.

Transition periods within family structures are part of nature's plan. Toddlers grow to bear infants of their own. The struggle is to keep the family shape a circle. Adult relationships among close kin takes hard work, good will and a lot of luck. We ask ourselves how can anything that natural be so difficult? Well no pain - no gain!

CALL ME MADAM

I represent countless older grown-ups who share my particular pique. We do not give BANK TELLERS, GARAGE MECHANICS, HEALTH PROFESSIONALS, SALESPEOPLE, permission to call us by our first name.

It is patronizing to be on a first name basis with young strangers. What makes them think it is friendly? It isn't. It is intrusive. We are not personal buddies. We won't share a Thanksgiving turkey at their place or mine. There is no relationship between us.

I have invited children as young as two to call me Grace because they have a place in my life. But those dealing with me in public places are not entitled to any intimacy. When one is at an informal social function, introductions by first names might be suitable despite age differences. I doubt, however, graduate students would be comfortable calling the dean of their university Joe, Sam or Mary even if they are at Grandma's dinner table.

It seems particularly tasteless to address people unknown to you by a first name in a business or professional situation. It can be insulting or downright foolish. I understand the trend toward less ritual tradition as an effort to make less space between status. It's fashionable among celebrities and politicians. President Carter wanted to be known as Jimmy Carter rather than the more stodgy James. President William Clinton is known as Bill. It is their option. It also may be a showy bit of theater. I'll bet that unless one is related by blood or marriage, a present or former president is addressed by a formal title anyway.

If Barbara Bush left a message for some reason, would anyone who didn't know her call back with, "Hello, Babs?" I have contacted administration offices of banks and grocery chains. They are amazed that I complain. Name calling of customers is supposed to be a hallmark of personal attention. OK. but if the goal is warmth toward the consumer, how about using my full name? No one has to curtsy but I prefer a little respect to pseudo cronyism.

PERSPECTIVE

Worries of yesterday are hard to remember when today threatens our tomorrows. A serious earthquake is guaranteed to bring all prior problems to an immediate halt. Survival is our first priority.

My in-laws were grateful to arrive in America after World War 11 with their limbs unharmed. They even managed to salvage a few family heirlooms from the London blitz. When I married into this family, my mother in-law and her two daughters re-distributed their treasures to include me. When I confessed to them that I was too nervous to dust the vase an ancient relative had brought to England from Japan a few hundred years before, my mother-in-law, Amelia, ordered me to enjoy it. "It's just a valuable thing." She said. "It isn't worth one of your heartbeats." I was reminded that "A damaged heirloom is not a fractured spine." I know clever people who cannot distinguish between calamities and the ordinary rumbles of life which leave us bruised but unbroken. I try to accept friends who have a different rating system than mine. My friend, Emma, puts me to the test.

Recently my car was towed. A terrible nuisance certainly. A catastrophe? Nah! While I don't have enough financial security to be cavalier about an unexpected expense, I have enough money to bail out my car. What I really resented was the wasted time. I had to call a cab, ride to the car kidnappers, fill out the forms and phone Emma that I might be late for her dinner party. She was only upset for my inconvenience and assured me that any time would be fine. But when she heard about the financial cost for retrieving my car, she was distraught and said " if I had to pay this kind of fine I would die." I hope not. Emma is a nice person. There are better causes to die for.

THE GOOD NEWS

It was a lovely surprise to learn that my weekly column had its share of young readers. Good on you. You are going to be one of us one day. You can hardly wait. Right?

Well, it's not so bad. When I was in my thirties someone told me to put Vaseline on my eyeglasses, stuff cotton in my ears and wear mittens for a day in order to preview aging. It would prepare me - it only depressed me. Good thing I reserved my opinion of aging. Most of us see and hear all we need or want to.

To claim no deficits as we grow older is foolish. Energy is diminished. The most agile among us struggle to maintain motor skills. Detailed notes of what to do, where to go and how to get there are vital.

Given all that, lets hear it for the advantages during our prime. Life gets easier. There are no time clocks. Each of us sleeps to a natural rhythm. No one is in charge of our comings and goings. Rich or poor, little or a lot, money is spent at our discretion. We have minor responsibilities and major privileges.

But don't rush it. If there were a contest the pearl of youth would best the golden years in a walk. I am merely saying what the great Yogi Berra always knew. The ball game "ain't over until its over". Just watch your diet, your waistline, and world peace. The coming ninth inning could be the one that evens the score.

HAPPINESS IS A THING CALLED JOE

I am not one of those who believe that everything happens for the best. Random misfortune visits most of us at one time or another. It is my nature to assess the balance sheet with an eye to recovery.

Survivors find purpose in life even if they have to manufacture it. Who knows? A new script could hold unexpected pleasure. Not our first choice of what we hoped our days would bring but worth it. Paraplegics wheel their chairs in special ballets and in basketball games. They understand that only the pursuit of happiness is guaranteed us. The concept of a natural right to that unnatural state is a late twentieth century fancy.

They have enough calories to sustain them. The proverbial half-cup is full.

A RHYTHM TO HIS DAYS

Most of us would love to love our work. Alas, we only like it well enough to earn our living. And so when we inch toward age 60, we anticipate long, tranquil years of uninterrupted weekends. Some of us were disappointed.

Those who lusted for retirement found that their identity was wrapped up in the business of business. "I had high hopes for my leisure years," my friend Milton reflects. "Instead I was amazed to find that I was exhausted from trying to fill my days and still felt half-empty all the time."

Milt now has a steady part-time job as a bank teller. It is ideal for him and a bonus for his employers. Corporate America has discovered the new but older employee who is able to play a significant role in the work force. They are reliable. They no longer have ambition fever to move up and out. Contrary to folklore, they are more patient and accepting of employee training with its rules and regulations. In addition, The Department of Employment in California discovered that the absentee rate for older employees is impressively low; as a matter of fact, lower than the figures of the younger set.

Milt retired as vice-president of a major manufacturing firm, but even for him the extra money is nice. Most of us could use additional dollars in this financial climate and for several older job seekers it is necessary. They must have additional funds for increased rent and medical costs.

It is cost-effective for private industry to offer jobs to retirees without providing profit-sharing or health benefits. Government agencies, educational institutions and community leaders are now willing to sponsor programs bringing together older employees with prospective employers. A practical liaison of mutual benefit.

NEVER EVEN

There is a difference between being a user and making use of. It isn't even subtle. To make use of people in our modern world has historical precedent. The West could not have been won alone. Most often barns were raised with neighbors. Mothers birthed their children with the help of those near enough to midwife. Pioneers didn't have to be friends to make use of each other. It was called survival.

Today business colleagues resemble our pioneer ancestors where we are bound by a common goal rather than affection. Exchange of favors is standard procedure and although friendships sometimes develop, it is not an end goal. If the interaction is jointly beneficial, that's good enough!

Is giving without thought of return a nobler concept? Probably. I supply apricots from my trees anticipating nothing. Melissa makes jam and gives me some. I am surprised and we are both delighted. When my waistline grows a size or two, my skirts and jeans are handed down to Carol's daughter who can or cannot return a favor. Peter got me my first client just because I needed a first client and his neighbor needed a competent professional. Delighted to be useful to both of us, Peter never expected gratitude from either of us.

Being used and being useful is not a mathematical equation. I'll never be able to level the mountain of favors Eleanor has quietly done for me. In turn, I have supplied Jean with my late sister's car and a near-new couch because I had access and she needed them desperately. Jean accepts and doesn't expect to repay me. She knows I got pleasure from filling a few holes in her life.

Best buddies can't always respond to our most urgent requests. That's fair. They would if they could. There is a fundamental principle within close relationships. We have the right to ask for anything but must be willing to accept refusals without rancor or loss of love.

As we age, loss of independence ranks high on our list of dreads. Inability to do favors for others frustrates us. We try to keep in mind that give and take is an old, honorable condition. In our latter years, we give what we can and take what we must.

NOT IDEAL - JUST BETTER

Some of us longed to make the world perfect. None of us did that. The bright and the able managed to improve their teeny piece of it. They took interest in community projects, supported educational programs, and voted for the politicos who espoused plans to improve the lot of the poor and disabled.

More commonly, us ordinary folk struggled in unremarkable jobs for decent monies and reasonable living spaces. The generation which followed were encouraged to do better. We hoped they would have the smarts to fashion the ideal.

Better educated and affluent, our kids managed to plug a few holes in the dike. On close observation, however, they seemed to have polished the surface around the holes rather than plugged them. The legislative graveyard is filled with the skeletons of proposals made but unimplemented. Appearances were big to the generation who wore designer jeans.

Maybe our search for a flawless society is a mistake. Easier to say we are doing it than to do it. It may be human to lie, cheat and stick beans up our nose when the expectation is Nirvana. Maybe the most recent crop of young citizens should focus on excellence. Not the illusion of it. Nor the results of it. Just plain commitment to do their best.

Quality of effort in and for itself as a basic goal can achieve more than ego satisfaction. It could bring an intrinsic self-esteem. Champions among us are not promised money or applause. They earn the gold after years of labor and many a fellow contestant is proud just to have been involved in the process. The idle or careless don't get rich and famous. Of course hard work and lofty ideals do not carry a guarantee either, but it is a good investment.

The latest critical thinking is that self-respect provides a climate to consider others. And that attitude is contagious. Those who witness it want it. They may not love their neighbor as much as themselves but close enough. It is sufficient. There might be an epidemic of altruism, integrity, and human growth. Not a perfect world. Just a new and improved one.

KNOCKING ON WOOD

The mother of a dear friend died last year. I had known them both for more than 60 years. Sleep-overs at their house included a casual supper that mother made just for us. Simple fare that I can still taste. I can also see her as she was - so pretty but fidgeting with some unseen anxiety. She always pressed second helpings on us to reassure herself that she had performed her culinary duty.

Our families have been separated by several states for decades. It was only recently that I had visited Chicago and was able to spend a few hours with my friend's mother. She had remained a pretty woman but I was distracted by how her hands continued to wring themselves in a constant state of dread. At the time she was reasonably healthy, financially secure, and surrounded by a loving family. My impression was that life was better to her than she was to it.

She gave me a pair of earrings that day we met. I remember thinking how generous and loving she is. I am sad for all those years she wasted anticipating some misfortune while only life happened to her. Bumps and lumps we all inherit by inhaling and exhaling. I wish she had given herself permission to wrench some joy from life.

THE BANKRUPT SPIRIT

On a recent visit to my home town, I spent an afternoon with a dear childhood friend. During the half-century that separated us physically, we managed to keep current. There were letters, telephone calls and occasional face-to-face reunions. Our individual benchmarks were acknowledged with grief or pleasure.

Our lives had been predictably different. As teenagers, we were miles apart in interests and pocket money. I could not afford to share her passion for shopping and fashion shows. Nor did I want to. My extra dollars were spent on stuff like theater and ballet tickets, events that made her eyes glaze over.

Strangely enough we neither judged nor envied one another. We accepted our differences and our relationship remained close. I admired her sense of style, she respected my love of learning. We even took advantage of our special interests. When we were high school seniors, I was glad to help her write required essays; she was pleased to hand finish a skirt for my sewing class. Fair exchange. We both earned A's and enduring lessons. To this day I can hem an emergency rip and Jane is more expert than I in unraveling those mysterious explanations the world of finance sends to clients. I rarely use a needle and thread but now Jane must truly understand the language of economics.

She went from a comfortable home provided by parents to one furnished by an affluent husband. His will recently provided for her to live handsomely for more than a hundred years. And still, poor thing, she suffers from the terror of poverty. She is convinced that should she be somehow stripped of financial security, she will be instant breakfast for jungle lions.

I am not critical of her dependence on fiscal wherewithal. It simply makes me uneasy for her. She is more valuable than the sum of her parts. I wish she knew that. Jane is one of the most genuinely good persons I have ever known. It is her fear of insolvency which impoverishes her.

I mourn for those like Jane who manufacture or anticipate personal disasters. To imagine the hot breath of dragons must be as painful as the real thing. How awful to be preoccupied with the possible worst. That is a good way to miss some of the best.

PARTY HATS

There is no loneliness like being among merry makers when a cheery posture is mandatory. For years I played Lady Grinch ignoring Christmas Day and New Years Eve alone at a Pantomime Show in London, the Vatican in Rome, a theater tour in New York etc., etc., etc. I am not unique. Millions taste emptiness at holiday time. My flights were just an escape from my vacant hearth and an unwillingness to share other people's decorations. These were good trips which distracted me and I came back refreshed and buoyant.

Lately, the urge to bolt has left me. Sadness no longer mark national celebrations. I still avoid ersatz gaiety but I now go to quiet gatherings where the company and food is dependably good. Only serious milestones continue to propel me into space. My 60th, 65th and 70th birthdays were spent among strangers who wrung no formal commemoration from my unwilling spirit. But other birthdays noted among those I love and who love me have a sweetness to them. A testimonial to my endurance through the years.

My ability to share recordings of events with others is still limited. It would, however, take a shriveled heart to be unable to share one's life in the altogether. I am glad to announce my kinships are deeper, wider and higher and I am pleased to be more grounded.

MEANING WHAT?

This writer is very shaky on some definitions. The entire country seems to agree on what wimp means, except me. Is my amiable neighbor next door a wimp because he refuses to take a stand on any issue until he examines all sides of a question? Is the blowhard across the street not a wimp because he has immediate opinions on everything?

I also struggle with words like sensitivity. I always thought that this word described a perceptive person who is careful of the feelings of others. I have known people with less tact than wasps, who claim they are sensitive. Maybe the word has a double meaning so it can also include those with teeny egos who are unaware of hurts beyond their own.

I find the phrase "I can't afford it" confusing. It is certainly a straight forward statement. No one could challenge a decision based on no funds. But it can also express an attitude. It is possible "I don't want to spend my money on that" would be a more honest response. It isn't easy for me to distinguish the penniless from the currently strapped by conversation alone.

And then there are the synonyms created to disguise the authentic. Milk, for example, has twelve different names on food labels to confuse the allergic among us. There are, of course, hundreds of legitimate new words born every year. When one adds "Micro" to "scope"," wave" or "chip" the meanings are changed. We can all agree on those definitions.

I am offended by those who confuse childlike with childish. Particularly if either of those terms are used to describe older adults. True there are people who remain childish their entire life. G. Bernard Shaw is often quoted as having said "Some people grow old before they grow up". And then there are some lucky Senior Citizens who are childlike. I share that gift. We display unbridled enthusiasm for the unexplored. There is no end of things to see and learn. I am giddy with the wonder of life.

A RELUCTANT ROMANCE

No longer young, I've grown jaundiced. There is no reason to trust the mechanical tyrants who have taken over our planet. Among the most suspicious is the computer.

It is Nanny to world banking. My own financial accounts, health records and grocery bills are all controlled by people feeding numbers into a system. These people rely on the accuracy of the machine. They, themselves, may never have learned to add or spell.

To my shock and horror, I now live with a computer. I never even dated one. This is a dilemma I share with many senior writer friends. Fingers grown stiff often need an automatic aid. Thousands of us creative types now must admit that once we have conceived the word, we can't reproduce it without the meteoric speed and legibility of the computer. And I would be small-minded indeed if I didn't also confess that my writing life has been rescued by my computer's ability to produce spell-check, correct punctuation and provide a thesaurus. Sure there are resistors who are using their 8 & 1/2*11 pads, rigid typewriters or ancient quills. The rest of us have succumbed to the ease with which word processors are able to put down our words.

Some people use software to play bridge or compose Bachian sonatas. Writers don't care. I don't want to master anything more complicated than a self-cleaning oven. It is embarrassing to admit I have assigned human properties to the computer. "It" loses texts, has sick spells requiring a computer doctor, and sabotages verb agreements.

I have grown dependent on my machine but have no hopes of becoming user friendly. No matter, we are wed forever. Locked in a love-hate embrace until death do us part. My only comfort is that I am going to outlive the so and so.

AN EXACT DIAGNOSIS

Medical schools might consider offering a course called "I Don't Know." Not a semester. Just a course. As it is now, some physicians are loathe to admit they haven't learned what our symptoms mean and treat us by trial and error. Patients must share the blame for this dilemma. Most people insist upon definite answers to what ails them. They admire a medical person who can recognize an illness and prescribe methods to cure it with complete certainty. Always. Even when there is room for question.

Clinical puzzles are studied in laboratories by scientists until pieces fit well enough to become a discovery. Pasteur's crowd must have pitched out a lot of sour milk before they found out that sterilization would make it safe. Sometimes what is common medical practice gets discarded for a better therapeutic method only to return at a later date. The re-entry of that medical dinosaur - the leech- is brand new again. This once extinct mode of therapy, is now being used in spinal cord injuries.

Lately there is mounting evidence that the medical community is examining modalities of disciplines other than conventional models. Although, Osteopathic Doctors have been given traditional hospital privileges for some years, Chiropractic, Naturopaths and other trained health professionals are now being accorded some respectful attention. Many MDs are recommending some homeopathic procedures and medications.

The new population of the aging American has created a health education event. The United States boasts 55,430 people over 100 years of age. The Census Bureau estimates that one-third of the population will be over 65 by 2010. Young physicians are now being trained to treat older organs. There are already techniques which promise to improve or heal our rusty parts. Surgery is now available to replace hearts, livers and joints.

I try to be aware of actions which may be timely for me. A promise of good health from the health experts is not a guarantee but I do not accept an out-of-hand "What do you expect at your age?" from a physician. It is no longer an appropriate analysis for a disorder that needs relief.

I don't pretend to understand the enormous complexities of the human body. But there are lots of plain language resources for the non-professional. I try to make sure my unfamiliar data comes from periodicals which document facts instead of hype. Strange cure-all magazines aren't reliable. Neither are the back of cereal boxes.

I want to be informed enough to ask intelligent questions. I don't expect my doctor to know all the answers. I just want medical people smart enough not to pretend they do when they don't.

CROWDED AT THE TOP

The Sandwich Generation is now a club sandwich. The 1990 census figures project a population of more than 100 thousand centenarians in the United States by the year 2010. This means that four generation families will no longer be rare. Five living generations are already a growing phenomenon. "Children" will become elderly within their parents' lifetime. Today's sturdy 80-year-old can have both a 100-year-old parent and a 60-year-old offspring who has a college age grandchild.

Libraries and book stores offer a plethora of material for parents in almost every stage of life. The exception? The relationship between older generations. Their interaction is fraught with confusion. Sixty year old juniors will continue to covet the approval of an 80-ish Mom or Dad. That's natural enough. No matter how successful we become in the world at large, we want above all to make our 80-year-old parents proud. And no matter how important and rich we become our aging parents still expect a little homage from us. Our hundred-year-old grandparents may demand all younger generations pay court. It is tricky when families now have three elders in direct accedence. All of whom were born into starkly different generations and locked into different conventions.

Each era brings seismic transitions. Evelyn's 97- year-old

mother, Fannie, remembers the miracle of radio. In the 1940's Mae West was barred for life from that medium because she played the role of Eve in a drama co-starring Charlie McCarthy. Charlie was forgiven because dummies were exempt from sin. Sixty years after those innocent days, television has brought nude strangers into my living room.

Plane travel was the advent of my generation. It was able to introduce me to bits and pieces of an America I would never had known otherwise. Now the computer age has introduced another new way of life. Corporations have employed people to work at home in order to reduce traffic congestion and office space. Sophisticated machinery keeps the work flow moving from residence to job place electronically.

Those are just a few examples which caused huge societal tremors for all us. Generations remain 20 years apart but mores are redefined every 5 years. Certainly the almost 21st century moms and dads who are enjoying role reversals are a mystery to the elders. Their granddaughters who have a full time profession can be thought to be violating their family obligations. Their grandsons who are in charge of home and hearth are considered ne'er-do-wells. Parents in their 80s and above can also be very judgmental about the nine-year-old grand and great granddaughter who wants her ears pierced. When her big brother puts a hole in any part of his head for decoration, he can expect some pained reaction from the aged relatives.

Although mores change with the speed of light, I believe morals remain the same. My personal definition of morality is kindness, truth, and honor. Universal staples except that politicians and preachers of each era are eager to stamp their own subjective MORAL endorsement on everything and every body. Four and five layer families also have different versions of what is honorable. During my youth, divorce was thought to be a miserable disgrace.

Today a daughter of a friend who has never been married yet has two much-adored children. One born out of wedlock, one born as a result of a sperm bank. My friend applauds her daughter's courage in defying convention but no matter how much the children are adored all the great-grandparents are appalled at the manner in which they were conceived.

Until a handbook is provided on how to negotiate the conflicts within the bloodlines, I would suggest a little statesmanship. It's a much respected discipline and learnable skill. Even all three levels of grandparents may be willing to participate in the exercise. During delicate but caring interactions, the older generations may find the modern ways of the younger members strange but not necessarily evil. The younger group may consider some traditions of the elders worth preserving. At the very least there will an effort to exchange feelings and ideas in a loving climate.

As for me, I am not nostalgic for what was. I simply want to know how to deal with what is.

The Plateau

PATCH, PATCH, PATCH

Recently, close friends have been invaded by body snatchers. Me too. While we were busy congratulating ourselves on our youthful spirit, our anatomy was doing the mazurka with a demon called Maturity in the Extreme.

True, there are still contemporaries in the neighborhood who are hearty. These people see a dentist or a doctor only on rare occasions. Boy, are they smug! They suggest that decline is our personal penalty. We must have indulged in mindless deeds and impure thoughts.

Not necessarily so! Most of us were virtuous in thought and tended our bones with respect. Marion is a first rate person. Her living habits were almost perfect, yet she had to have a clogged heart valve replaced. The Rev. Smith had his cataracts removed. Actions taken to prolong and improve their lives. And it has. Marion had her surgery ten years ago and is living long enough to experience male pattern baldness. The good minister can read perfectly but his hearing is not what it used to be.

The political world certainly demands stamina. Yet several famous United States Presidents became elected to office despite terrible infirmities. Franklin Delano Roosevelt was confined to a wheel chair. Jack Kennedy had suffered a broken back and Addison's disease. In recent years, we had an 80-year-old who had two cancer sites removed surgically, and an assault from a would-be assassin's bullet. He recovered to be a helpful model to the aging. Whatever your political beliefs one must be willing to admire his capacity for conquering personal accidents and disease.

Millions of ordinary folk overcome barriers to a more or less active life even when it seems as if our body parts have to take a number for service. Our physical problems are dealt with on a priority basis. Primary organs take precedence over bunions.

We heal and return to whatever is normal for us. Normal could be for us to surrender the vigor of youth. Victory is to be able to do this gracefully.

FRANTIC

My Aunt Edna is a busy person. Her calendar runs on full because she is very good company. Only her close family knows what frames her social life. Raw terror! She believes that unless she flings herself into the world with all her body parts moving, they will dissolve into helpless disuse.

Not all Aunt Ednas in the world are fighting inertia. There are lucky people of all ages who have lots of natural energy. They hunt for new experiences like miners pan for gold. Their taste for adventure seems boundless.

That is not Aunt Edna. She coffee cloches every weekday morning with someone she sincerely dislikes. Many an afternoon she calls me to complain how much this person bores her, yet she depends upon this alliance because it gets her up and out. She tells me that if she ever remained at home she would take to her bed.

The afternoons are filled with anyone available. Since she is charming, attractive and clever, people court her company, but should someone have to break a date due to illness, she will get a replacement immediately. My aunt uses her apartment to shower and change clothes. She is a perpetual house guest hither and yon with whomsoever.

Why do I question the texture of her life if it works for her? Well, it seems to me that all that animation suppresses her undercover depression and loneliness. I pray she takes some real pleasure from her comings and goings despite the obsessive nature of it. It's as if she gulps the time left to her without savoring any of it.

A BUDDY ALARM

I know how to protect myself from my enemies. Adversaries rattle before they strike. It's easy to dodge venom when you are warned. But when friends say "I want to tell you something for your own good" - look out, it's too late to duck.

Heaven save me from those who mean well. The claim that they wouldn't hurt me for the world sounds hollow when they say things that sting. I wish some dear friends would stifle themselves before they comment, criticize or condemn my march forward to a new frontier. I understand if my move to a place foreign to them seems bizarre. They are not required to applaud my efforts as I fill my own gaps but it is mandatory they hold the cold water.

It takes enough heart muscle to leave companions without them chipping away at my resolve. I am prepared to risk a mistake. I have yearned to live in the Northwest for more than a decade. Granted, it seems strange for a Cosmopolitan like me to suddenly relocate to where no one knows my name. But there it is.

People who had no reason to doubt my competency asked autocratic questions and pronounced edicts. "Who will you call if you get sick?" "You are not healthy enough to go off alone." "Have you thought about how much you won't fit in with country folk?" "How will you cope with that cold climate?"

Well, a few years have gone by now and I have been sick, cold and among strangers. I knew poor health could be managed. It only took a call to a doctor and I recovered. A housekeeping service furnished some personal necessities. I don't mind being alone during the tough times. My old friends were missed for their companionship in the good times. I miss them still but the change in seasons delight me and the country folk accept me.

Not all my friends were so negative about my plan to transplant my roots. I see now that those who were so openly hostile to my leave-taking were expressing their own fear of the unknown. They did not share my longing for mint fresh experiences above possible peril. When my transplant was even more fulfilling than I had hoped, the naysayers were pleased but never came to visit. My supporters called often, made vacation itineraries to pass through my current nest. They also made trips just to see me.

I never replaced the warmth of these old friends. I didn't expect to. New playmates filled only some of the blanks. Yet the Northwest is ultimately where I belong now.

When I need hugs from those I love and an urban fix, there are airplanes.

Life is not ideal here. Life is not ideal anywhere. Ever. But at my age, there is enormous pride in giving myself permission to improve the remainder of it.

SILENT MUSIC

My younger neighbors have said to me, "Dad is not interested in anything since Mother died." My nephew confided to me, "Now that Mother is alone she is so depressed." The parent who is newly quiet may be cause for concern but need not be ominous.

While it is possible that inactivity can be symptoms of depression, it is just as likely that Mom or Dad are just doing what he or she prefers to do now. Sometimes the surviving spouse has always been sedentary. The departed partner could have been the one who created the social stir.

Now when people have only themselves to consider they are free to choose a slower pace. The mother who entertained constantly is satisfied with a TV dinner. The father who escorted his wife to all those charity balls enjoys his solitary fishing.

Loss of spouse is a brutal shock. Part of the ordeal is to establish an individual identity. Critical to the process for some is stillness. This may be an interlude. Or not. In any case, it should not always be mistaken for despair.

Our society places a premium on high energy. We tend to equate animation with good health. Only the infirm are allowed to be inert. Albert Einstein and Isaac Newton were considered dim. Or melancholic. Why else would they sit in silence? To figure out the world; that is why. I may not contribute to the understanding of the universe but it may take the same time and concentration to figure out my particular place in the world.

Once active I now sway aimlessly in a hammock. No need for my young neighbors and relatives to wonder about me. I am not depressed - just relaxed. It may be nature's plan for me and I approve of it.

USE EVERY DIGIT

What is old? Football players are old at 35. Knees betray them. Most cover girl models have had it at 28. Cheekbones have short careers. Scientists, composers and writers, educators and politicians seem to go on as long as they like. The brain can continue to improve for a lifetime.

Research now indicates that people past 75 years of age can be as nimble-minded as their 40-year-old counterparts. Comparative studies over a thirty-five year period demonstrate that IQs do not diminish with advancing years. To the contrary. Healthy, older people amass a lot of information so when they repeat an IQ test taken years earlier, their scores actually improve.

I thought that wisdom would be a natural companion of aging. I figured it would compensate for the loss of bone mass. Not a fail-safe equation. Enrichment depends upon our continued interest in knowledge. The phrase "use it or lose it" has never been more apt.

Gerontology centers which study alertness among the aging population have determined that those who maintain interest in a contemporary world will live a longer and more wholesome life. That's what keeps our machinery oiled.

Exposure to new facts, opinions foreign to our own seem vital to growth. Partners in seats on airplanes have exposed me to the joys of chicken farming, bee keeping, and the problems of sports writing, forestry preserves as well as secret dramas.

Oh yes! A post script to this report. As we age, reflexes often falter. At 75, time constraints of IQ testing must be lifted for accurate results. The older viewer is unable to punch the buzzer in time on Double Jeopardy even when they know all the answers. Younger people are quicker. But not necessarily smarter. So there!

SURVIVING THE PUNY TIMES

Some of us get unlucky. Nature has a tantrum and we are felled. Several years ago, I joined an army of people who needed help with a splintered carcass.

After my physician, the physical therapist was my second stop on my road to improvement. Blessed be her name. She taught me how to reshape and strengthen my muscles. I also needed special techniques just to get around my house and so a professional lifeguard was recommended.

These wonderful people are known as Occupational Therapists. The title comes from the days when they tutored things like Basket Weaving to keep the institutionalized occupied. Today, they are the experts on how to compensate for physical handicaps so that we may perform normal tasks.

They know how to remove the daily obstacle course from living spaces by rearranging furniture so that every room was made stumble proof.

I was taught methods for using a variety of homely devices already living in my household. A lowly sponge, for instance, gives leverage to weakened fingers, so that wrapped around a knife, a pot and a mixing bowl, I did some light cooking. A similar tractable item wound around a toothbrush or used to turn a doorknob makes one feel more able-bodied.

There are a variety of formal appliances available for maneuvering the body with more ease and less pain. The Arthritis or Osteoporosis Agencies have each fashioned a catalogue itemizing mechanical gizmos which make patients functional. In addition, the medical supply business is a growing industry which can supply appliances to help remediate every physical flaw.

My health has returned but, nevertheless, I continue to use the back-protector the Occupational Therapist molded for the driver's seat in my car. My steering wheel is padded to eliminate slippage. I have a specially crafted reading chair which supports my lower back. I own a metal book holder, an orthopedic pillow, and my air filter is in constant use. These items increase my comfort.

If a puny time ever strikes again, I know a thing or two for sure. Number one is that it doesn't have to last forever. Number two is that there are handy inanimate friends out there waiting to improve my lot.

THE UNLOCKED DOOR

At a certain point our social lives jell into a comfy mold. We enjoy a circle of friends with whom we share common interests. Our basic needs satisfied, we are content. Additions to our network are rare. Understandable. New relationships require effort.

But every now and then fate flings us together with strangers. A cruise, a local college class, or a high school reunion, will introduce us to someone we find stimulating or visa versa. Anecdotes so familiar to our cronies are once again amusing and insightful. My reputation as a raconteur could be reinstated.

More happens. Just meeting someone who holds different political or religious views enriches what is important to me. Fresh information does not contaminate sacred points of view. To the contrary - I am energized by people who attract me. Personally, I have seldom met anyone who has changed my vote by new and improved data. But having my opinions challenged by those I respect, inspires me to evaluate my own stance. My philosophies may not change but they could be deepened in a more thoughtful frame.

My own clique might not provide that. We reinforce each others long-held convictions on everything. In fact we are rather smug. Reappraisals are painful. Rooted ideas are permanently valid.

We oft-times either criticize or ignore a changing society. We don't try to understand our possible role in it.

It is reassuring to surround oneself with those with whom we have a history. I have no plans to discard old friends. It's comfy to have shorthand communication with them. How nice it is to be with our mirror image. But somewhere along the way looking out the window provides a broader vista.

WHEN IT'S OVER, IT'S OVER

There was a family wedding last month. When the pictures arrived, an unattractive old lady sat in their midst. I was about to ask who she was when my nephew said, "That's a good picture of you, Aunt Grace." That young man risks his inheritance.

I would have gone into deep mourning had not some friends told me that these pictures didn't do me justice. They could see that the pictures made my eyes look small, my nose look big and my smile crooked. These people had known me from girlhood. There is something precious about those who still see the young woman in me unchanged by time. This is particularly touching among older couples. They don't notice each other's sagging chins, receding hairlines and lines that form slowly through the years, as strangers do.

I miss my youthful face. Although it was not beautiful, it was pretty enough for special attention. In my twenties, I wanted to display my intelligence above my appearance. It was the beautiful but dumb era. I resented being thought of as merely handsome. In my thirties, however, my intellect was verified by a college degree, professional status, and a bonus of good looks. I am still pleased with my appearance but what does one do about cameras?

Then I remembered some early famous beauties around my vintage who do not seem to appear in public any longer. Has anyone seen a recent photograph of Loretta Young, Claudette Colbert, or Doris Day? Only Katherine Hepburn seems to have made peace with her image as a feisty crone. She claims she is no longer vain about her appearance. Her pride is in who she is becoming as a person.

Well, me too, Katherine. After all we had a long run as glamour girls. After the initial shock, we give up the mantle graciously.

STOIC LESSONS

Born of good intentions, all parents and teachers make unintentional blunders. My seventh grade science teacher taught the value of four food groups which have since been declared unhealthy by modern nutritionists. My mother taught me not to cry.

When I was a small child with reason to wail, she would embrace me and croon a gentle "don't cry." Maybe she thought that if I stopped crying I wouldn't hurt any more, or maybe she could deny her own pain for me if I did not cry. By age ten the crucial lesson was cast in stone. I had learned that it was shameful to shed tears. Outsiders especially must never know there was anything sad in our family. It was a disgrace to admit to family illness, poverty, divorce or any other less than elegant circumstance. So I entered the family conspiracy. No one suspected how really poor we had been during the Depression. No one was told about my brother's 10-day jail sentence for a boyish prank and my sister's divorce was treated as a military secret. Our posture of public composure was nailed into place.

My mother admired dignity above all else. When my brother went to serve in World War 11, she wept silently in his arms for only a minute. An hour later she calmly hung a wash in the backyard flanked on either side by other mothers whose sons had already left for battles. These mothers brooded openly every day to anyone who was near by. My mother did not discount their torment but she would have rather appeared heartless than naked.

I was my mother's excellent pupil. I met personal disasters with no display of hand wringing or screaming. Like my mother before me I swallowed tears until they formed a private drowning pool. Certainly not a therapeutic exercise but wonderful professional help was more available for me in my own middle years. I managed to skim off the top of my grief in confidence.

No doubt, repressed emotions can affect the immune system but I am convinced that unresolved feelings were not the cause of my bouts with cancer. As a matter of fact, I think my recoveries were quick and complete because I concentrated on regaining health instead of screaming.

Time and distance have given me a new understanding of my mother's passion for impassive reserve. During extreme distress, it gave her courage. Me, as well. Many a times a posture of strength has furnished me with the spirit to survive. There is an appropriate time, however, to disclose one's wounds to friends who feel shut out by denial. Maturity and some good professional counseling brought the realization that earlier trauma and body defects did not make me a defective person.

I had a wonderful relationship with my mother. She had a native wisdom and a wonderful humor. She was a comfort in my youth and a friend in my adult years. It's too bad my mother thought it such a failing to reveal herself as vulnerable. I wonder why my mother did not trust people enough to take support from them. She gave enough in her life. I remember her as a thoughtful neighbor, a sensitive friend and a respected member of the community. That was real enough. Only her pride was false.

A TALE OF WHOA!

I learned to drive a car almost 50 years ago. Since then, I have driven a million miles or more earning only three citations for minor traffic violations. But despite my competent history, it is sobering to know that one day I may become a menace on the road. I can only hope I will recognize that day. Already there are a few clues clamoring for attention.

My peripheral vision is no longer automatic. I have to remind myself at each and every crosswalk sign to look both left and right. My clear right of way must be confirmed and not assumed. After dark, oncoming headlights seem to emit a glare so bright that they make me night-blind. Moreover, I don't always hear car horns. Even when I do hear them I don't know if they are honking at me.

Those of us with worn-out eyes and diminished hearing want to deny a few obvious symptoms that would challenge our ability to navigate. Automobiles are our life-line to an outside world. It is a terrible loss of personal freedom if we are unable to control our coming and going on our personal schedule.

Yet all of us need to be totally honest with ourselves about newly formed problems. Statistics from the United States Department of Transportation indicate that persons of 60 years and older have the most frequent fender benders. We may not go far or fast but we do the most damage. I believe this. Even a careful driver might not be able to avoid the careless ones because response times become slower for most of us past 60 years of age.

Driving is no longer as robotic for me as it was in days of yore. During my younger years, I could sing along with the radio or have a vital conversation with a companion. Today, I now need my full attention for the road. And so I make a few promises to myself in order to protect both me and my neighbors on wheels.

1. I shall plan to travel during the times traffic is light.
2. I shall plan to dodge busy intersections.
3. I shall not drive in areas which make me uncomfortable.
4. I shall budget enough time to arrive at appointments. (There is little that causes more anxiety than tardiness.)
5. I shall never drive after a sleepless night. (This drowsy condition is subtle but can cloud our driving perspective seriously.)

There are 90-year-old sharpies who remain entirely proficient on the highway. Others hang up the car keys much earlier. There is no legal requirement to do this unless we cause a fatal accident. There is no obligatory test for license renewal either. To the contrary. After passing an initial test at The Department of Motor Vehicles, it validates our license by mail forever. This places a burden of responsibility on senior citizens to assess their own driving skills truthfully. The American Association of Retired Persons has comprehensive self-help tests available for the asking and also conducts classes to improve deficiencies.

Some of us admit to a few new flaws and take steps to mend our ways. We try to become more vigilant without becoming a creeping danger to drivers behind us. We get to hang on to our car keys for a long, long time.

PARTNERS

We are not a huge graying lump hobbling through our remaining years. We are not excluded from the problems of the world. The big picture includes everyone. We are spared nothing. Acid rain drizzles on all living things.

The quality of public education touches us privately. Not only as proud or disappointed family members. The unschooled are most often unemployable. Aging citizens are prime targets for mugging. Unaffordable housing is fraught with unattractive possibilities. Grown children unable to maintain their own space will clutter ours.

We continue to be part of the life force. What happens in ballot boxes affect us directly. Not all legislators love or honor their aged relatives. There is no law that they have to. They are bound only to protect our civil rights and human needs because we belong to a community they have pledged allegiance. We periodically remind them of our interests in the voting booths.

DOWN BUT NOT OUT

Even the heartiest person is unable to win every battle of germ warfare. Life experience has taught me that I am not immune to skirmishes of bodily harm either. The manner in which I recovered was a vital lesson. It was OK. with me if I was temporarily frail. It was not all right to feel defenseless. With a bit of research, I discovered there was lots I was able to do despite being unable.

A survey of my neighborhood revealed some immediate resources. A local pharmacy delivered a few goodies along with the life savers. There was a market that carted grocery orders to my door. In a pinch taxi cabs were available to pick up and set down for a modest fee.

I never knock money. It gives us greater options for means of assistance. Bigger financial resources does not always, however, make the difference between passing and failing health. There are community agencies servicing rich and poor alike. Hospitals have Social Service Departments that provide some critical information. Mine told me which agency delivered the hot meals, and which could provide transportation to the doctors. They had a roster of people who were available to run a crucial errand.

The Visiting Nurse Association supplied me with home health aides to help with bathing. The Red Cross had more than coffee and doughnuts in their bag. It was their nurse who changed dressings for my wounds, checked for infection and dispensed medication. Similarly, the Public Health Department does more than control epidemics. Their offices were another referral source for goods and services.

My Congressperson was a bonanza. There was a Senior Citizen specialist in the office who knew about the ways and means of healthcare benefits. It is amazing how many inexpensive or free services are out there when you know where to go and what to ask for.

We cannot always protect ourselves from bad times. But we can try to make them tolerable until good times roll our way again. "Hope for the best and be prepared for the worst" is more than an old bromide. It's good advice.

HUSH

I remember the stillness of my childhood. The long, quiet summer mornings broken by muted sounds. A breeze which carried laughter from a hide-and-seek game down the block. My mother humming in the kitchen. All sounds were events. Clear. Separate.

I mourn for that placid era when we took the time to saunter through our muffled days. But population growth and industrial progress nipped at our heels along that quiet promenade. Automobiles clog our streets, airplanes rage above our heads drowning out the melody of rain on our roof.

We are becoming a tone deaf people. The volume on passing car radios is loud enough to disguise their tunes. The portable ones attached to a youthful grip are known as boom-boxes which assault us in the streets with their high fidelity.

I know many things of my childhood are illusions remembered through a veil of time. But I clearly recall the tranquillity of another age. A time which allowed my thoughts and feelings to rise undiluted by invasive clamor.

It is hard to find composure in a hyperactive society. I try to recapture serenity that comes only in moments now and I strain to hear birds sing. I sometimes find myself responding to the outside excitement and bustle out of nervous habit. It is as if any repose or hush would be a final one.

THE FALL OF A KNOW-IT-ALL

Automatic wisdom was supposed to replace youthful arrogance. It doesn't happen. I hear people screaming for a return to tradition as if they had known the truth of things.

They remember the family, the town, the country that looked happy and solid. Ergo there was a time when we were both. They forget the core was sometimes hollow; problems stuffed into a Fibber McGee closet.

Perhaps those who advocate the standards of yesteryear confuse morals with mores. Customs change. Ethics do not. Yet we continue to mistake one for the other. I guess it is safe to say that stealing, lying, killing are immoral anywhere any time. And so which traditions shall we return to? Public hanging? Which old fashioned values should be reinstituted? Slavery? We worship vintage appearances despite historical proof that no social dictum of yesteryear protected us from villains. Attila the Hun was no deviant. Lizzie Borden lived in a good neighborhood.

This generation has birthed more cultural changes than any since the caveman discovered fire. Too early to assign the facts a letter grade. But different is not automatically inferior. Rigid family structures of yore have also produced its share of deviance. Labels of "dysfunctional" and "co-dependency" are recent in an attempt to understand human behavior. But those actions were recorded since Cain killed his brother.

Maybe latch-key kids will be the model for self-sufficiency and honorable deportment. Maybe not. Only one thing for sure. Once the pen has writ, it moves on. No one advocates a return to a monarchy or a totalitarian form of government once having experienced a democratic way of life.

And so when we moan about the values of the good old days, I wonder. When was the last time there was peace on the planet? And how come not?

MOMISM

Cats, dogs, and pandas experience parenthood. Most of them nurture their young. Infants are suckled, toddlers are taught who is on their food chain and how to avoid those who would make a feast of them. Tiger and lion moms figure they have done their part by birthing the cubs and then teaching them survival skills. That's natural.

I have heard that some members of the animal kingdom eat their young. Yuck. But I have met a few Human Being mothers who also ingest their infants. Mothers who don't want their children to live apart from their maternal innards ignore a primary parental lesson. Give children the tools to make them self-reliant adults.

I admire my neighbor Rachelle who knows that. She was a stay at home mom until her son was six whereupon he went to school and she went to work. She would have preferred a secure profession such as school teacher or accountant for her son but it was not his choice. He became an actor. She takes pride in his talent but more importantly she applauds his courage in pursuing a hard career where few will ever know fame and fortune. His pleasure is in the creative process. Stardom escaped him but she is grateful that he found enough work to have provided a home for his family and college education for his children without her advice or financial help.

On the other hand, Marion's son is barely more than a pauper because few classical musicians are little more than solvent. Even fewer are acknowledged publicly. She is delighted that her son is blessed with private joy even when he is without an audience. He manages to pay rent, to keep warm, dry and indebted only to his art. Marion thinks her adult child is one of the lucky ones who has a love for his work.

Claire is not a worldly person and if she had her druthers her children would be heterosexual. After some chest beating about whether her early training influenced their sexual preference, she accepted their homosexuality as normal for them. Claire is close to her three gay children. She prays for their continued good health and doesn't obsess about "might have been" or the "what might be". It is agreed between them that homosexuality does not make her or her offspring inferior. Her children have good health and loving life-partners.

Other Homo Sapien mothers who have no place beyond home and hearth guard their superior role by showing and telling their offspring how to think, feel and perform. When children begin to think, feel and act in ways alien to the teacher, they are baffled, hurt, and angry. It was as if their investment has not paid dividends.

These are the parents who expect a weekly appearance, daily phone calls and announcements of movements in advance as if their approval were required before trips and business decisions. They chew nails when middle-aged children travel. These parents have not grown beyond the first junior high prom night when waiting up could be considered appropriate.

Rachelle, Marion and Clare validate the particular uniqueness of their children. As long as their children were worthwhile, honorable people, they are gratified. What they treasure is the individual growth spurts their young ones took without mother's advice and consent. They take a minimal amount of credit and little blame.

STORM WARNINGS

Everyone is an authority on child rearing. It is a wonder Dr. Spock was able to make a living. He, as well as other experts, has been grossly misunderstood. The Permissive Doctrine was so badly mangled that the very term is out of use. I think permissiveness meant that adults did not have license to bully smaller family members. Kids were entitled to thoughts and feelings of their own and even a vote. Surely it did not propose we indulge a child's every whim. And at no time did the advocates of a permissive environment believe children were exempt from restrained and considerate behavior.

Clearly people of all ages must have boundaries. It makes us feel safe. It is especially frightening for youngsters when what is allowable is fuzzy. Naturally, families differ. Good manners are stressed at the Smiths whereas the Brown house emphasizes religious ritual. Some might say those goals have little in common. After all, the criminally insane can master the concept of please, thank you and attend the church or temple of their choice. The tone in which we preach values is vital. We do not teach our young so that we can impose our superior power.

Certainly there must be rules. Our home is our castle, and heirs apparent shalt not trash it. While some parents don't mind rubble confined to a child's domain, others forbid a closed door mess.

The dictum that children should be seen but not heard has been handed down from generation to generation. Dialogue is invited in certain households. Others will tolerate none. Negotiation is reserved for State Departments. Children follow orders or else. Else what? Plenty, depending upon family discipline policy.

It is possible we have all experienced some form of child abuse. Bruised bodies and broken bones are ugly, visible signs of harm. But neglect or indifference can sting enough to do lasting damage. And serious name calling or persistent shouting, can also qualify as mistreatment.

There are occasions when a raised voice is appropriate.

Youngsters can test patience beyond endurance. Common sense and protection of parent sanity demand we teach children certain behaviors are not acceptable to us. Yet our sense of proper conduct for instruction of children is merely opinion. Not etched in sky or stone. The best in human relationships are among people who know they don't know it all. And despite the fashions that come and go, families in a democratic society would do well not to have tyrants in their home. Of any age.

Abused children will molest their own young. Almost always. In addition they are likely to attack their aging parents. There was a recent expose in the New York Times on incidences of assault on the elderly at the hands of their adult children. As the population continues to grow older, grown children have a rare opportunity. They can express past rages they endured helplessly as youngsters.

When our offspring become adults who make us proud, we are not too shy to take a modest amount of credit. When children disappoint us, we blame peers, social conditions and our in-law's genes. Maybe all of it is true. What could we have done to make the difference? Possibly everything.

WHO ASKED YOU?

Someday, someone, is going to blacken one of my eyes in the aisle of a supermarket. I am moved to respond to a whimpering toddler imprisoned in a shopping cart and who is warned by an exasperated parent to shut up. These very small children stop crying when I tell them "I know, it's tough to be a baby." They don't know what I have said but somehow they know from my tone that it is sympathetic. They seem to need understanding as much as they want freedom. The parent on the other hand doesn't feel a bit fraternal. I get an occasional "mind you own business". I tell the child of these testy parents "Some day you will own a car and you don't ever have to visit them." One of these mamas or papas is going to punch me out.

Oh well, it will have been worth it. A crying toddler could use some mild intervention from a "because I said so" type parent. When I see older children being shaken or really belted, I speak to the manager.

Of course, I also see some very good parenting. Shopping expeditions which take place after lunch and nap. Little ones whose energies are directed in helping pick a can from a lower shelf when they are mobile enough to walk and tall enough to reach; who are made to feel shopping is a fun family recreation. A harmless enough lie. Grocery shopping for most of us is a drag-and-a-half.

BUZZ WORDS

Mothers hear the faintest whisper when their young are infants. It is a universal phenomenon. By the time children reach teen-age years, mothers have learned to tune out. Each generation speaks in secret code. Just as we manage to break it, the younger child develops a new one. A common language is rarely used. These times are reserved for emergencies. The use of the family car for example.

Soon our kids have kids of their own. Our children are appalled. Their progeny have a vocabulary which is all too understandable. Words once scribbled on bathroom walls have found passage in everyday prose. Us older folk are less shocked. We already had our jolt when our middle-aged solid citizen children were the young ones who discovered the "art" of rock concerts. They brought Shakespeare's Elizabethan expressions back into the mainstream. But then these same free-wheeling hippies became the doctors, the lawyers and the senators of our nation.

Of course, not all our flower-children grew into valuable folk. There were tragic casualties. People damaged forever by the currents of social transition. It was always so. The flapper era of my parents time also produced its share of victims. But not as many as world wars or the Great Depression. So lets chill out.

Linguistic experts have made a profound study of how language evolves through common usage. 19th century men of letters would not understand our ads, written or otherwise. Modern authors who struggle to preserve our grammar must ultimately lose the battle. Sorry Ed Newman, James Kilpatrick and Rene Jacque Cappon. Traditional use of the English language does not protect a civilized society. Contemporary speech merely reflects a now environment.

That ancient wag who said "sticks and stones can break our bones but words can never hurt us" knew better. Insults are painful. Hearts break. There can be ugly scars. Do obscenities do that? Not hardly. They may reduce and corrupt the speaker. Not the listener.

DENOTATIONS

My older sister and I were never close friends. She was ten years older but the gap was deeper than the decade between us. Even as adults, we defined our world in polar opposites and although we made a sincere effort, conversations between us were garbled at best. Yet, ironically, it was she who gave me a book on my eighth birthday which governed my communication skills forever.

This book was no ordinary fairy tale. Yes, the story was about the usual king and his marriageable daughter. This particular king, however, had a special requirement for an eligible suitor. The criterion for the competition was deceptively simple. Suitors must find two words with the exact same meaning. The king was determined that an heir apparent to the throne be able to express regal policy with absolute accuracy. Many young men of the village offered two words they thought to be identical. The king would then reject them and explain the distinction.

That fairy tale read by me at 8 made me mindful of precise expression. The notion that words carry subtle differences and the power to shape ideas was not lost on me. Not then and not now.

Adjectives in particular are treated gingerly since they are the words that carry the value judgments. Dumb used to mean dim-witted. Nowadays we know that those who are mute are physically handicapped not mentally deficient. We continue, however, to describe the provincial, the unsophisticated or the dense as dumb. My neighbor is truly unschooled. Her fourth grade education limits her reading ability. She had never heard of the famous quotes "To Be or Not to be", or " …Where Ignorance is Bliss, T'is Folly to be Wise." But once she said to me, "Dying is easy, living's the trick" paraphrasing poets Shakespeare and Gray. My brother-in-law has a higher IQ than I do but continues to reinforce ideas formed at puberty. Despite his Ph.D. in science, he could easily pass for stupid.

Genius is often considered eccentric at best. Einstein, Galileo, and George Bernard Shaw were a few whose behavior was unconventional enough to be thought weird. The brilliant Oscar Wilde was jailed for his unorthodox love life. And ordinary people who enjoy borcht, egg foo yong, baklava or fried okra can be thought to have strange or exotic eating habits depending upon one's geography.

Since we have graduated beyond grunts to express our emotions and thoughts, we are convinced we communicate them. Instead speakers say one thing; the listeners hear another. The fairy tale king illustrates this phenomenon when he finally accepts two words which he thinks are exactly alike. But "Finish and Fini" have a separate language base. The author can be excused, however, since fini has been integrated into our English vocabulary.

My sister and I never did manage to share the same language. I am convinced at this late date (a) she didn't read the book before it was given to me (b) she chose the book because she thought it was a grammar lesson. No matter, I am grateful to her. It is a pity we never found a way to bridge the gorge which separated us. In the end, I found no words to comfort her. Maybe holding her hand was enough.

MUZZLED

I lie a lot. Unless I am actively bleeding people expect to hear "fine, thank you" as a response to "How are you? Almost everyone past age 60 has some persistent health problem. My body's peccadilloes are not fit for human conversation. Other than my physician, no one wants particulars.

Yet our health is the first topic I and my special cronies engage in when we are out to lunch. After a half-hour or so of comparing symptoms and remedies, we acknowledge our embarrassment over how much time is spent discussing our ailments. One of us will say, "can you believe this? We are talking about our bodies!" We remember a time not so long ago when we listened to our old relatives describing their innards in detail. None of us could imagine we would ever be reduced to this kind of babble.

And so, although the motto for thousands of us is "never explain, never complain" frankly, I am thrilled to know those of my kind who can empathize with my aging process and the common diseases and arthritic conditions. There is an advantage to this routine of course. We tell the world we are fine and we begin to believe it. But give us a break young people. Solitary confinement is a bitter sentence if we fall short of being permanently cheery. Even the bravest among us must be allowed a tiny whimper now and then. It is normal. Honest!

IN RETROSPECT

When my siblings talked about our mother and father I didn't
know who they were talking about. My father was a gentle,
scholarly emigre of the last century. He made me proud. His son, on
the other hand, remembered him from the pain of disappointment, a
father who could not recover enough from the Great Depression to
give his heir either financial or emotional support. And my sister's
father was a saint.

I know it is unfashionable, but I recall my mother with loving
warmth. She was funny, intelligent, and smart. I enjoyed her
company and valued her counsel. I didn't always follow it but it
always made sense. My brother's mother built him a pedestal. It
made him dizzy enough to fall in failure. My sister's mother was
competition.

Reality reshapes itself through the years. We add or subtract
our individual nightmares. What is left is called memories but seen
through sentimental layers the past becomes distorted. Those of us
who kept journals are often astonished at what we read years later.
We record the truth as we experience it, only to misremember it later.
I trust what was sensed at the moment. Feelings have an integrity
beyond time which can cloud the facts. History teaches that exalted
public figures are defamed decades later. With few exceptions.
George Washington, F.D.R. and Ike all had their posthumous lumps.

When the smoke cleared, they were no less great. They had simply
taken their places among us mortals. Imperfect.

Now I am making memories for others. I will be recalled in
mosaic-like fashion. Or in isolated pieces. My reputation in the
hands of whomever is reminiscing. An adoring or critical survivor. I
would like my descendants to remember me accurately. I want them
to realize my apparent dismissal of thrift was a zest for living in the
now. I want them to be glad I didn't borrow money. My strong
opinions were not edicts no matter how formidable they seemed to
others. I want to be family famous for my wit and insight.

Our dogs should be in charge of our epitaphs. They are
objective. They understand unconditional love.

CHRONIC IS BORING

Almost anyone responds to a crisis. Acquaintances telephone and send clever, cheery notes. Friends provide the necessities during a major illness. They haul you back and forth for medical attention, shop for perishables and stock your freezer. They also discourage gratitude. All they want is that you mend well and rejoin the lively.

The wise patient begins to relieve the loyal troops during convalescence. One assigns minor but urgent tasks to non-intimates who had volunteered a feeble "Is there anything I can do?" in the past. One may ask a neighbor to add an item or two to their own shopping lists.

Good! So far your friends are devoted and you are considerate. Everyone expects "normal" to return reasonably soon. But suppose "normal" doesn't return for a long time? Or never? If you think you are disappointed wait until you hear from your friends. Friends can be seriously frustrated.

Despite their best efforts, you are not what you used to be. They may still be your beloved friends but you are not fun anymore. You cannot participate in hikes, golf matches or attend outdoor concerts. They are concerned about you. But when a crisis becomes a condition, drama turns to tedium.

Eager phone calls which chartered your early, steady progress turn to check points. Questions are disguised statements. "How are you feeling?" can be a demand that you better feel better and you better say so.

You are now showered with endless advice. "Change your diet, change your doctor, get more exercise, get more rest." They insist that you try harder to reach good health. It's the American Way. The emergency is over. Now shape up and get well.

Even so. Potluck dinners continue sporadically. Friends continue to be concerned about you. That is, until beach and picnic weather set in. If you are still not sturdy enough to join them, expect disengagement. That's reasonable. How many people want to remain on intimate terms with a perpetually temporary invalid? One cannot blame them. They want to smell the roses while they are able. They don't want to gather moss at your house playing Trivial Pursuit especially if you always win. If you are so smart - get healthy!

It was your turn for resentment. After all, you have been the model of courage. You deserve attention. You are outraged. Particularly because in your heart of hearts, you are most angry with yourself. Your body fumbled robust. How embarrassing! And beneath anger and embarrassment are their close companions, fear and hurt. Fear of being alone and helpless. Hurt because no one cares enough. These feelings are strong enough to make a lip of iron quiver.

All feelings being fair, you are absolutely entitled to yours. The big question is what are you going to do with them? Your friends are struggling with their own scared feelings. They don't want to be reminded that vigorous is tissue-thin. They want to ignore their own prospect of any personal infirmities. So who and what will provide you with comfort? What course of action will bring relief from pain and a return to some pleasure?

Perhaps you could make a list of all the things you have yearned for but never had time to do. After one lengthy illness of my own, I made such a list. What appeared on the paper really amazed me. My list did not contain one "should" or "must" do. It was spontaneous wishing. I did not consciously know I wanted to learn bridge or take piano lessons. I also did not know that I needed the quiet of solitude to mend my body. This may not be true for others. They may need as much excitement and as many people as they can gather. Whatever. The main idea is to live according to your individual needs and to the limit of your capacity.

I made friends with a different life-style. A stationary bike ride in front of the television set replaces those excursions along forest trails. Ping pong replaced tennis and I learned to pitch horse shoes rather than bowl. There is no limit to what one can do when one is unable to do.

I had already experienced major changes during my lifetime. The advent of menstruation, a driving license, my first kiss marked the end of my childhood. My first paycheck was an introduction to adulthood. My first gray hair was a sign that I had begun THE aging process. But it wasn't until a bout of diminished abilities which threatened to render me childish again did I have that growth spurt to maturity.

Reduced capabilities did not render me hapless or friendless. Those I love and enjoy have accepted my persistent disabilities. We enjoy time together wherever and whenever we can and I am pleased to report my lust for life remains hale and hearty.

RESPECT REQUIRED

As my brother grew high enough to reach his father's kneecap, he though his father was shrinking. He referred to the future as "when I get big and you get small."

By the time he was 10, he caught on. No matter how big children grow, parents remain grown up. Many of us forget this when our parents become elderly. We self-appoint ourselves guardian making a lot of assumptions which are often wrong. Father may not always know best but unless there is dementia, he generally knows what is better for him.

It is tempting for some children who are strong and solvent to try and provide for their parents long before it is actually warranted. That could cause hurt feelings on both ends of the spectrum. Parents might perceive the offerings as an affront to their independence. The offspring are offended by the rejection of their good intentions.

Even when a parent's condition requires the help of children, the parent should have the vote and veto power. Somewhere in this world there may be an ideal family where Mom and Dad can define their approaching problems, admit them voluntarily to eager children who are just waiting for the appropriate time to be helpful. I don't know this family.

Most of us have to remind ourselves that no matter what befalls our parents, they are always full-grown. Should they become infirm, they are still adult people. They may become our responsibility but they never become our children. And so we tread gently. The need for mutual respect is never more vital.

HUMANISM IN A HI-SCI WORLD

In the 11th year of my life, our 6th grade teacher told our class it would be impossible to reach another planet. Why not, for pity's sake? Lindy had already flown across the Atlantic Ocean. Buck Rogers was visiting Mars in our funny papers.

Ms. Kramer gave us a well-informed, rational explanation. We could never invent a plane fast enough. The airships would have to be large enough to house 100 years' worth of fuel and spawn four generations of people. The class bought that image.

What did Buck Rogers know that educators did not? Well, if necessity be the mother of invention, imagination may well be the father. We realize now some cartoon strips are more than fantasy. Science fiction is more than escape literature. They pose serious questions. Serious scientists provide answers.

Well, now we have space travel. Is that exciting or what? This was a critical question being debated at water coolers and Senior Centers everywhere several years ago. One point of view was that exploration of space was motivated by hunting for war maneuvers. We were testing the feasibility of new war weapons and developing surveillance methods against potential enemies.

These opponents to the cost of NASA operations thought

monies should be better spent on food, shelter and healthcare for the poor. The older citizens remember when the duty to feed, house, and clothe the human family was basic. We never fully met these obligations. The ideal was to try our best. Have our technocratic sons and daughters abandoned this priority?

Those in favor of inter-space travel claimed investigation of our galaxy would reveal secrets which would improve us earth-bound mortals. There is some evidence of that already. Examination of human beings who have been in space programs has been significant in the treatment of heart disease. Fire-retardant clothing was developed. Laboratory clinicians cannot predict what they will unmask. Dr. Fleming's forgotten sandwich developed mold which led to his discovery of penicillin. Many scientific revelations are born out of happenstance.

I am willing to admit personal ignorance. Surely, the interspace telescope is exciting and I concede its promise. I am convinced that these forays into the now not known will reveal data which will offer new understanding about the human bodies. But somehow I hope the explorers will bring back intelligence to disclose how to enrich human nature. Until then, we must continue to do it the old-fashioned way. In our own neighborhood, our own city, and within the borders of our world.

THE ETERNAL PROGRESS

Since the days we lived in caves, the younger generation needed to do their own thing. They respected the elders who taught them to set traps for their prey but the quicker, more accurate bow and arrow was probably invented by some smart aleck adolescent.

There is no stopping the enterprising youth.

Improvement is their job and I say terrific. My home is a glut of labor saving devices. I don't want to beat my clothes clean with a rock. My mother would have loved my dishwasher. My father would have adored shaving electrically. Surely, a microwave oven, a food processor and a VCR improve the shape of my days.

But as youth simplifies our lives, they complicate our world. The creation of the computer leaves me gasping. I am stranded on an island with no access to the internet highway. Naturally all that hardware must change the human experience. I am told that worldwide communication between strangers on E-mail will promote rapport among people within nations. That's fine for those who can afford the machinery and speak computerese. I worry about those who are excluded from this experience. I also worry about those who are computer literate and isolate themselves from human contact. Already there are reports of couples who met through computer correspondence and married without face to face meetings. No more unconventional than mail order brides, I guess.

It is just that this fast forward button might advance us toward a giant wasteland where we ignore the constants that must increase in a civilization. Kindness should be beyond trend or technology. Peace is another. Despite the wars fought in its name, we must continue our search for bloodless harmony. And we certainly need humor more than ever in these robotic times. Laughter in and for itself has been in every land since the earth cooled. There is no survival without it.

Maybe the young of our young already know the elements that must be in our society to elevate it above the science in it. Wouldn't it be wonderful if when its their turn to better the world they manage the ultimate. More important than any invention before it. A way to affect human nature so that we automatically care about ourselves enough to care about each other more.

BETRAYAL

Everyone loves gossip. The National Enquirer has a bigger readership than the best-seller book list. Most of it is mean, dishonest and low comedy. But respected magazines also print interviews about the rich and famous. We are fascinated by celebrities. Just knowing spicy news about them makes us feel part of an exclusive club.

Curiosity seems instinctive. People may not want to know their neighbors but they want to know about them. My own vital statistics are available to anyone who asks. I disclose my age, my income and my calorie intake to strangers. Intimate details I reserve for people who are   permanent in my life. They know when and if I dye my hair or have a love life.

Then there are the rare people in my life to whom I reveal the scar tissue which covers old psychic wounds. These friends know that just by giving pain a voice it becomes bearable. I feel honored when it is my turn to listen to them. How good it is to feel safe with people we trust. The matters we discuss are between us and no one else, ever!

Friends often separate, particularly later in life. Interests change. We move away. But even when our friendship has lost its knit, our secrets are sacred. Forever! And that is the way it should be. Let the tabloids do the dirty work.

HAPPIER BIRTHDAYS

Aging is not a disease. It is a process. Babies can depend upon bone growth at a predictable rate. The skeleton of those of us beyond middle-age is not so precise. Our bones decrease in bulk and strength with infinite variety.

Once upon a time the family doctor told patients "aches and pains are to be expected when we get older." It is still common for practitioner and patient alike to dismiss treatable disorders as natural signs of aging. But aging can no longer be considered an illness. While it is true that older people are prone to particular health problems, there is no uniform diagnosis. In 1988 the National Board of Internal Medicine finally recognized Geriatrics as a certified medical specialty, at last, and not a moment too soon. Every week 210 people will celebrate their 100th birthday within our borders. By the turn of the century there will be almost 100,000 of us who were born in 1900, by 2050 there will be a million centenarians.

We've got to make this longer life-span worth living. Knowing some medical facts could influence the state of our future. It is vital to place your trust in those health professionals who are current with the latest gerontological discoveries. When we get an early diagnosis and treatment we can reduce the effects of a new health problem significantly.

I have been pronounced cured from episodes which were once considered terminal. I was willing to accept a partnership in my own healthcare and learned all I could about my own condition from second medical opinions, text books and professional volunteer groups. Most doctors welcome informed patients. It makes their diagnosis easier and a treatment plan more effective.

Cooperating in our own healthcare is quite unfamiliar to most of us. We can't spell or pronounce a lot of what is wrong with our bodies. But then how many of us can read a stock market page or understand the world of real estate? Yet none of us would deny we must know enough to invest in a home and buy a safe bond or two.

There are a few lucky octogenarians who participate in marathons runs. The rest of us are pleased to move our chassis to the neighborhood emporium for our necessities and recreation. Whatever the boundaries, they sometimes have plastic walls. And so - one, two, three, PUSH!

The Descent

UNTIL THE FAT LADY SINGS

It is not inappropriate for me to consider the end of my life. I am already too old to die young. Nature will one day recall my body; an event too ordinary to be named tragic. Sad only for those who will notice my absence and a grim reminder that nobody is exempt from an earthly leave taking. The moment of departure is the only unknown.

Given this unavoidable fact, one understands why we have an intense appetite for good living. Definitions of the good life, however, are as unique as fingerprints. A quiet river to fish by for some, a season ticket to the Metropolitan Opera for others. Whatever! There are also countless among us who just want to do whatever they do forever.

Every couple of years a guru appears with fool-proof methods for additional decades of hardy living. So far none of these theorems survive clinical scrutiny and gurus espousing immortality turn up their own toes sooner or later

At this writing, fat-free diets and aerobic walking have been sanctioned by both the faddists and scientific community. Seems promising. The claim is that proper nutrition and exercise will guarantee longer and healthier life. Three cheers for better health. If ice cream deprivation will improve my hearing, and pumping iron will energize me, I'll invest my time and effort. But a promise of longevity? I don't think so!

It is my opinion that no amount of wheat germ or push-ups will shield anyone from a due date. I assign a lot of credit to my ancestors for how and when my mortal coil dissolves. I realize, however, it is not all a gene pool lottery because there are indeed destructive habits that can provoke an early call from the Accountant in the Sky.

Smoking, excessive use of alcohol, inactivity in the extreme and wars, are behaviors which might underwrite a premature demise.

In 1984, the Stanford Medical School conducted a twenty year study of identical twins. The analysis indicated that life-style plays a significant role in medical results. One case study, for instance, followed the medical history of male twins. The findings were typical. Twin A did not smoke, seldom drank, and played tennis regularly. Twin B was more than a moderate drinker, smoked cigarettes, was physically inactive and thirty pounds heavier than his brother. Each had experienced a coronary at 48 years of age. Twin A had a much milder attack. Twin B suffered extensive heart damage. At age 78 a stroke happened to both, A was able to be rehabilitated enough to learn golf. B was virtually an invalid. Both died at 83. Similar scientific surveys produces a definite hypothesis. Intelligent health habits many not necessarily prolong life; but they should make it better.

While I don't believe eating sensibly and jogging my brains loose will insure my longevity, I do believe that it will guarantee more carefree days. I am willing to walk a mile for quality time. My table manners have improved but don't anyone tell me that sweetened oat bran bars are as good as hot fudge sundaes. Never!

If I knew my death date, I would mix a martini, light a cigarette and bungie jump. But I don't. And so in the main, I maintain.

PLAYTIME

     I don't think Evie has ever openly lied about her age. She simply refused to discuss it. But lately she joined a group where they are taking tap dance lessons. "Retirement gives me time to do what I really wanted to do for years. It is as much fun as I thought it would be." I don't ask the average age of her classmates and she makes no mention of it. But she knows that I know with whom she is jumping up and down. Older people - that's who.

     My friend Kathy was, and is, a great beauty. During the summers, she lives on a bucolic island near the Canadian border. She is at home among the trees and her vegetable patch. During the rest of the year the spirit of that nature world remains with her as she treats the sick in her city environs. When my friend Kathy turned 70, she had her ears pierced to accommodate some exotic earrings. It was a signal to herself that vanity had not vanished with the advancing years. A nod to her still elegant radiance.

     Miriam became grandmother for the first time in her 82nd year. Although, she had not expected or yearned for grandchildren she is as thrilled as she is surprised. She continues to paint every morning. Her new model is the heart of her heart. Shirley wrote her first book for children last year. Norma is going on the Master

Bridge circuit. Eleanor is writing art criticism on the Internet for a literary magazine. Gerta is learning T'ai Chi. They are having a wonderful time.

I know just as many people who have no interest in fulfilling half-forgotten dreams or cultivating new ones. They are perfectly content with a day out for lunch and a movie followed by a night in for television or a good book. Their idea of calisthenics is wiggling their toes. They are not the least bit withdrawn, depressed or bored. They are satisfied with who they are and what they do.

Idle Americans are not our ideal. We equate passive elders with infirmity and uselessness. Centenarian mountain climbers are the heroes. We look to them for the right way to age. Well, I don't believe there is a proper code for aging but I do think there is a judicious course to being elderly. Any way you can!

The Big Sneak Attack

The hearty among us are shocked when their step is slackened, their hearing muffled, or their eyesight clouded. "The Sky is Falling, The sky is falling" screech these older Chicken Littles.

Even I, who had experienced enough past health glitches, was taken aback by natural events. Sure Uncle Harry is 93 and can hear a baby's whimper next door. Aunt Gertrude at 86 can still thread a needle without squinting. But what about those of us whose eyesight measures good on the medical chart but still need glasses to find our glasses? And our transfers in and out of a car is newly awkward for a once lithe body. Maybe the most traumatic is the realization that everyone mumbles. I find that I am constantly asking people to repeat themselves.

Time to acknowledge the prayer the addicted among us say to maintain sobriety. "God give us the courage to accept the things we must. Give us the strength to change what we can. And the wisdom to tell the difference".

THE PROVISIONAL BIOGRAPHY

I was asked recently to write my obituary for the local newspaper (a common practice for a columnist. Sound morbid? Well, it wasn't. It was fascinating. For one thing, the text had to be crisp. Since I was writing it, it would be unseemly to assign words of praise to my performance so far. Facts stood starkly alone.

As I sorted through the bare bones of my life, I realized how far I had traveled and how fast the trip. I had already met a primary goal or two. The quiet child from a Midwest town had made a small clamor in the Northwest. Noticed enough to warrant a public statement when she is laid to rest.

When others write our obituary, they catalog those items which seem important to them. Few of us get an opportunity to author that which we feel defines us most. I was free to mention my favorite projects and people in what may not be a final notice.

But I was also struck by how much was left for me to do. Toys and adventures set aside for a later date. Later does not last forever. If I ever hope to play the piano again, it will have to be soon. If my fingers lodge a protest, a flute might do. I want one more terrific train ride. I have never been on a cruise.

There are a dozen places in the United States I want to revisit. I want to meet one more friend before the following is printed.

Grace Lee b. September 22, 1924

Died .... at........from.............Her California colleagues will remember her as a Social Worker at the Laurence School, a Community Educator for the National Cancer Institute, and as Co-Director for Inter-Generational Services. She moved to the Northwest in 1989 where she wrote "As We Age" a weekly column for the Gannet Press.

She is the best selling author of *"On the Way to Over the Hill."*

Maybe one day someone will add a postscript between the dates where a tablet rests. "She did the best she could with what she had. Good enough."

WHERE ARE MY KEYS?

When my parents began to slow their pace, I was pleased. They had worked hard and long and if they now chose to sit and rock a bit - hooray for them. It was only when they suggested we go out for dinner one Thanksgiving that I realized my parents may have braked to a halt. Large shopping expeditions and extensive preparations were more activity than they could now handle. They still wanted to host the holiday parties, but could not. What used to be a pleasure was now a burden.

It was hard to see my folks exhibit signs that they were permanently less able. At times it made me more angry than sad. I felt betrayed when they who had been invincible became diminished. Few of us are mature enough to accept life's inevitable sad transitions without painful protest. Our parents should stand between us and our own mortality. But what really made me anxious was memory lapse. It terrifies most of us because we are convinced memory loss signals utter decline. Yet everyone experiences forgetfulness. Depression, anxiety and excitement all affect our recall. Once we are convinced that we forget more than we remember, fear about it adds to the problem. My friends, Gerontology specialists Drs. Jim and Sylvia Weishaus, claim that older people who exhibit forgetfulness had the same personality flaw all their life. They were probably the teenagers who were chronic losers of homework and tennis shoes.

With all due respect to my friends Sylvia and Jim, I have lately burned my share of pots for the first time in my life. Now a portable smoke alarm saves me from myself. Microwave ovens which turn off automatically are a favorite. Medication is measured into marked boxes indicating when to take them. If the contents are not there at the end of the day, they have been ingested. I also make sure all medications are compatible. Nothing can make more confusion than a prescription war.

I now know my parents were a good model for growing old as they accepted decline with as little fuss as possible. First aid substitutes were tolerated to help them hear, see and chew. They couldn't replace any human parts in those days but they made do with what they had with good humor and patience. I am now struggling with similar conundrums. And I forgive myself those blunders I can remember.

DEFICITS

Sometime in the middle of my middle age, my knuckles cracked. I hardly noticed it at first. The hands looked normal enough. It took me longer to shuffle and deal the cards at the bridge table but then my fingers were never what one could call nimble. Of late, however, they follow orders only on occasion.

These ten pincers let me know who is boss. Buttons are buttoned at their discretion. My cup aims for a counter but lands on the floor. I cannot grip an item as small as a pin or as large as a bowling ball. Me and my hands are not always dance partners. These extremities sometimes nap without my permission until I shake them awake.

Among my short list of virtues is my acceptance of what definitely is. Initial grief is allowed. Despair is forbidden. Regret is a thief that robs me of whatever blessings of gold remains in my vault.

No one anticipates the last season of life with excitement. There is no manual to prepare for it. Stuff just happens. Having an attitude helps. Mine is simple. If holding a pencil is hard, try talking into a cassette. Or go to the movies. Chocolate chip cookies are good.

Infirmities are not the exclusive property of the elderly. I am not singled out by fate to endure an exclusive affliction. I note that deficits in later years can be the result of wear and tear. Some of us lucky ones got a lot of mileage out of whatever joints are now worn and torn. Amidst the sorrow for what was, I find that soothing.

A MODEL FOR SENIORITY

When I met Uncle Ben, his middle years had already passed. He had outlived two wives and my aunt was his third. They were a wonderful older couple. Serene in their aging years. And despite some physical decline, I suspect it might have been the best part of their lives.

He was an uncommonly handsome man. Short and stocky with a James Cagney stride; but his voice several notches above a normal volume. Maybe that was because my aunt's hearing had faded or maybe he had been forced to shout above that large crowd of immigrants who entered this country in the early 1900s. I am sure he wore other signs from battles. In that transition I had never seen him without a smile. There was also a trace of stubbornness. Good on him. Tenacity was a must in order to hang on during the Great Depression.

He was not an educated man but he was smart. Yet no new world event could shake his lifelong-held social doctrine of Socialism. There are those who admired his loyalty to an ideal. Others secretly mocked his unshakable faith.

Uncle Ben's heart was damaged and he knew there were few years left. That fact seemed to relax my Uncle Ben. He felt permission to devote the balance of his years to maximum comfort and joy. There was enough financial security to satisfy a modest life-style. He loved my aunt with the ardor of a youthful suitor after twenty married years. He was almost courtly as he held her hand. His children were a source of enormous pride. And as with most grandfathers, he adored his grandchildren and had the time to show it.

Uncle Ben was in his eighties when he chose to endure a heart surgery that would lengthen his life without quality assurance. Although he supported the Right to Die movement, it was his personal preference at that moment to tolerate a restricted existence rather than none. He knew at the time of by-pass surgery that auto and plane trips and even walks in the park would no longer be possible but despite severe physical limitations, living was still sweet and worthwhile for him. And he carried it off with flair for almost five years more.

One of the very best things about my Uncle Ben was the way he died in his late eighties. A complete and authentic acceptance. No last minute appeal to the heavens. Not for him. Had he read poet Dylan Thomas's "Do Not Go Gentle into That Goodnite", he would not have approved. Enduring a physical decline of bodily functions that would have enraged most, he took his leave with peaceful resignation. And with more dignity than was ever afforded him before. He was a model for all of us who follow him.

MEMORIES

I remember when air travel was so new, passengers clapped as we landed. It was a "thank you" to pilot ability and gratitude to be on familiar ground. Now we merely look at our watches to check arrival time.

I remember my old school mates and neighbors clearly. We were clones of yesteryear. People who thought and acted like us were proper thinkers. Some of us didn't jell into the mold. We let the larger world in and now know all denominations, all colors, all genders and all political philosophies. How enriched is my now from my then.

I remember when gloves and hats were standard dress for young ladies. Gentlemen of taste wore hats winter and summer. The 4th of July required white shoes for females and black and white oxfords for males. Now only the most formal occasions insist upon a dress code.

A women who smoked in public was déclassé. Now with the present bans, the street is the only place for anyone to smoke. Lipstick was the hallmark of approaching womanhood at 16. Today, department stores have counters where children of any age are choosing mascara.

I remember when the doctor made house calls routinely and mail was delivered four times a day. Now only an ambulance will visit our home and we are lucky if the postman finds our address. I still have not recovered three weeks mail lost in a recent change of residence. Not uncommon.

While cooking was my hobby, I never baked a pie. I still have friends who pick berries fresh from their gardens in order to prepare cobblers from scratch. It is very good eating. Does anyone make their own fudge any more?

Refrigerators were once ice boxes and now they make their own cubes. Every actor on the Classic Movie Channel is long dead and children think milk is produced in a carton.

Only the very, very rich traveled to Europe. Now international business commuters as well as retirees choke the avenues East, West, North, and South.

The ancients thought left-handedness was a sign of the devil. In my day, it was thought a perversion to be corrected in the young - the sooner the better. In 1992, we would have elected a left handed person for President of the United States whether we had voted for George Bush, Ross Perot or Bill Clinton because these candidates were all left-handed.

Tattoos were once known as the property of low life. Now George Schultz, the former Secretary of State has announced that he has one the shape of a butterfly in a hidden place. How fashionable, George!

By the time senior citizenship sets in, we have a heavy investment in traditions started in our youth. Despite the explosive societal transitions since then, it isn't always easy. Some of us are outraged. The more forward of us try to separate chaff from grain in our already formed value system. We hear words on the 4 P.M. TV news we hope our grandchildren don't know. Some of our young people live together without benefit of clergy. These are a couple of conventions that no longer matter. I remember what was scandalous in my own youth.

My parents were sure that jazz was junk. But now there are jazz classics which rank with the old masters. True, my social security money is not spent on rock concerts but I realize it is possible for current rages to make musical history.

The automatic shift, master charge cards, grocery carts, and frozen vegetables are just a sample of things introduced during my life time. Thank Goodness! Nostalgia is a wonderful place to visit but I don't want to live there.

THAT LAST MILE

Simone de Beauvier (in her 1972 book *"Coming of Age"*) did an exhaustive study of aging from 2500 BC. Simone's considered opinion was that old age wasn't worth getting born for. She is supported by many philosophers including Ovid, Montaigne, Chateaubriand and Gide in her sour assessment of aging.

In our more therapeutic era, there have been advances in relieving the misery a very elderly can stumble into. Alongside birth, death is the most common stage in life. Physicians are the ultimate experts on dying. They learn about terminal diseases in medical school. They know the five components of the patient's process: denial, anger, bargaining, depression, and finally acceptance. Acceptance is hard for the healer who wants to control life.

Sherman Neuland, MD wrote a recent best seller entitled "How We Die." Dr. Neuland, a surgeon, confesses his part in a conspiracy to postpone death among patients long after they were willing to leave a life of suffering. He has bitter regrets that he encouraged his beloved brother to prolong treatment which caused certain agony and no hope of life without pain. Dr. Neuland warns us that many in the medical profession seem unable to surrender the battle to death who must ultimately win.

I am mindful that I too must join all those who lived before me in a grand finale. And like most of my peers, the burning question is when and how. Most would vote for an unconscious release of living. A sudden seizure while asleep in their beds, Not me, I think. Lately, I have formed a very personal decision. I would hope to know the nearness of the inevitable in order to experience my last breath as my life empties out. Preferably alone, because it is not an adventure one can share or recount anyway. That wish sounds strange - even to me.

Robert Frost wrote "Miles to go before I sleep." Midway on his life's journey, he knew that all creatures eventually die but he worried more about the length and condition of the road ahead than the final destination. Me too! I want to leave behind a used up life.

THE SPIRAL STAIRCASE

Compared to the climb up to this peak, my downhill path seems a gentle slope. I am in amazingly good shape for the shape I'm in. My heart, liver and spleen make no complaints. My arthritis is conditioned by water calisthenics, my asthma is controlled by wonder drugs and I have all my teeth.

My body is pleased to be less active during my days and cozy in my house most nights. Now that I am less propelled to fill my hour glass, I enjoy the easy pace. Picnics in the park have replaced my elegant dinner parties. And even then, I bring goodies prepared from take-out marts. Almost all of my clothes are ordered through catalogues and none of them have to be ironed.

I have not lightened my load in hopes of a longer sunset. I only wanted to divest myself from those "have to do" tasks that once defined my life. Now that I no longer have to justify my existence, I feel more intensely alive. I resemble an aging Alice in Wonderland sauntering through unfamiliar doors; exploring new rooms and encountering adventures. It was only last week I was introduced to the evolution of musical instruments in a class about the symphony. It is exciting to learn these new details to enhance my pleasure at orchestral performances. This is just one of the many creative programs sponsored by a senior citizen educational foundation named Telos from the Greek word fulfillment.

In my wonderland, I understand the Mad Hatter. Sooner or later we all scramble for that important due date. The Queen of Hearts doesn't scare me either. I know that my head must roll one day anyway. I find this strangely liberating.

I love this part of my life. It's mellow time. The dessert tray as an award for just making it through the necessary chow I was obliged to swallow. I linger leisurely over the succulent end of my meal. My furniture rarely gets dusted. No one notices.

The march toward this height took muscle. I make my way to the bottom of my trail with a sure-footed gait enjoying the vista on the way down.